I Can't Believe
We Live Here

I Can't Believe We Live Here

The Wild But True Story of How
We Dropped Everything in the States and
Moved to Italy, Right Before the End of the World

MATT WALKER & ZENEBA BOWERS

I Can't Believe We Live Here

The Wild But True Story of How We Dropped Everything in the States and Moved to Italy, Right Before the End of the World

MATT WALKER & ZENEBA BOWERS

ISBN: 9781088021255

©2023 Matt Walker & Zeneba Bowers

Edited by Barbara Schultz and Kristin Whittlesey
Cover photos by Zeneba Bowers

Published by Little Roads Publishing
LittleRoadsEurope.com

Table of Contents

CHAPTER 1

A Day in the Life

Autumn 2022

*O*N A CLEAR DAY AT SUNRISE, we get to witness a magic moment from the terrace of our tiny apartment: The rising sun illuminates the castle on the opposite hillside, bathing the pastel stack of buildings in a distinctive pink hue. The moment is fleeting, but it never gets less beautiful, and we never fail to reflect on how lucky we are to get to live here.

The early morning breezes from the Cimino mountain above us carry the hint of an autumn chill, but it's still mild enough to keep the terrace door open overnight. As I'm setting up the Moka pot for our morning coffee and Zeneba dumps out fresh kibble for our trio of desperate cats, we hear the sound of Sante's rooster, crowing in the paddock below our terrace. The rooster is joined by a couple of goats bleating. As if in response, the town's siren wails out across the valley, signaling the beginning of another beautiful day in this little town of Soriano nel Cimino.

I should say "our little town," since we moved here from the US three years ago.

Zen beckons me back to bed for a last little snuggle under the covers. Since we moved, and now that we set our own work schedules, we have really indulged in enjoying the mornings — a major shift from our life in the States, where things were scheduled pretty much minute to minute.

Hoover, having crunched some kibble, has just hopped up on the bed to sit atop the covers at Zen's feet. I pull back the down comforter and just start to get comfortable, when "DING DONG!!"

We had installed that doorbell almost as a joke. Since we live in a studio-type space with no walls, and the only door is to the bathroom, someone could knock on the door with a paper clip and we wouldn't miss it. But Zen liked the homeyness of an old-timey bell ring, so I replaced the previous institutional-buzzer one with a ding-dongy one.

I look over at Zen, who is scrambling to release herself from the prison of covers that Hoover creates when he plants the full weight of his 18-pound body at her feet.

"DING DONG!!!" again.

"*You* have to get it!" she whisper-screams as Hoover refuses to move. "I'm not even dressed!"

She finally escapes from Hoover's anvil effect and darts into the bathroom, her pink nightgown getting stuck in the sliding door.

"*Arrivo!*" I call out, trying to buy some time while I hop from one foot to the other, rushing to get my pants on, before lurching to the front door. It's only about six steps away, from the bed through the kitchen and breakfast nook which is also the "foyer" in this tiny home.

As soon as Hoover realizes I'm heading to the front door, he relinquishes his spot on the bed and bounds over. He insists on greeting anyone who visits, begging them for attention, while simultaneously trying to escape out the front door. I heave him up into my arms (remember: lift with your legs), and open the door to greet a *corrieri* holding a small parcel.

As always happens with this little routine, the bored, distracted face of the delivery guy breaks into a big smile after he lays eyes on Hoover — all-white, gigantic, with a flower-patterned collar adorned with two bells and a pink cat-shaped charm.

The guy hands over the parcel, and we exchange "*Grazie! Prego... Buona giornata, ciao, ci vediamo, arrivederci!*"

It's perfect timing. I close the door and the coffee begins percolating out of the Moka pot.

Over coffee on the terrace, we sort through the e-mails that came overnight, banging out a few responses and taking care of a few other items of business.

We hear the sound of a scooter below us. *"Ciao Sante!"* I hoist my coffee cup to our neighbor as he pulls away on his Vespa on the little dirt track. He looks up and waves back. (Who knows what he thinks of this large mug of coffee — a triple espresso with a bit of milk, but he probably assumes it, like myself, is an *Americano*.) He has already finished his morning rounds attending to his chickens, and feeding the goats and sheep that graze on the adjacent hillside.

"It's supposed to be clear all day," Zen tells me, "so let's pop in a load." Like nearly all of our Italian neighbors, we let the weather dictate our laundry schedule, as our "dryer" is the breeze across the clotheslines. We bump into each other as I stuff the little *lavatrice* with as much laundry as it can hold and Zen washes dishes at the kitchen sink. (The washer is in the kitchen — which, as previously noted, is also the foyer, and the hallway, which also is our bedroom, and ... well, it is a really small house. The bathroom is about the size of one you'd find on an airplane.)

I have some charts to write this morning — a couple of arrangements of opera arias for our little ensemble to play in a concert coming up next week at a neighboring castle. I sequester myself upstairs in the attic, while Zen juggles writing our social media posts and clattering around in our kitchen.

The aroma of her cooking soon wafts up the stairs tantalizingly. I'm highly motivated to finish the charts so I can come down and "taste test." It's her signature red sauce — a sort of mix of *aglione* and *arrabiata* — my favorite. (Then again, nearly everything she cooks is, at that given moment, my favorite.)

After an hour or so, I come downstairs and we hang out the laundry. Even if the forecast is clear, we have to keep an eye on the skies, as unexpected mini-storms can crop up from over the mountain. But today looks perfect, aside from the occasional dropped clothespin. Today is a good day — we only drop one, watching it fall to the dirt track three stories below.

While the sauce simmers, we unpack our instruments so we can play through the new opera charts and I can see what works and what doesn't — another taste test of sorts. Then it's back to the attic to make a few fixes and alterations.

The town siren sounds again. Is it noon already? We close the computers and the instrument cases to take a lunch break. Zeneba puts a plate together — a bit of local cheese and a cup of farro and bean soup she made the day before. The siren is a big part of the rhythm of life in this town, and we've become accustomed to it.

After lunch, we wash the dishes and I head back upstairs to resume working... And then comes yet another sound of the rhythm of our life: a guttural *"Grhogh... Grhogh... Grhogh..."*

Cat owners will recognize my efforts to render that sound in print. That telltale sound, like a crappy scooter engine with a weak battery trying to get started. *"Grhogh... Grhogh..."* It alerts us to the impending disaster of a cat barfing.

I turn around wildly, scouting the upstairs, as I hear Zen leap up, her phone hitting the floor, as she yelled "No, no, NO... NOOOOOO!!!"

Then a sickening splash and splat as Socksie unloads what seems like her own weight in liquified cat food, spraying it from her favorite vantage point — halfway up the staircase.

Unlike our old house, where the stairs were flanked by two walls, here in our Italian home it's completely open — just a set of stairs in the middle of our open space, leading up to the attic. The upside of this layout is that it creates a nice airy space, full of light. The down side? No walls to contain spraying barf, and no safe way to run up the stairs to grab a cat in the middle of a "barfisode" (as Zen aptly characterizes this event). So we both just stand by helplessly, watching Barfocalypse Now and reflecting on the many romantic and glamorous aspects of our life in Italy.

After the clean-up — we have it down to a science, unfortunately — it's back to work. I pack up my cello and take out my guitar — there's not enough space for both to be out at the same time — to practice a couple of country-blues songs. Such is the nature of our musical offerings these days. We think our neighbors probably find it strange, as well. The sounds of Johnny Cash and Elvis must seem out of place on this idyllic Italian hillside, and all the more incongruous when we alternate it with 400-year-old Italian baroque music.

Around 15:30 (3:30 pm, that is — we're still trying to get used to the 24-hour mode of timekeeping), we get ready to head out to do our food shopping, now that the shops in town will be reopening after their lunch break. Again, living in Italy requires a bit of an adjustment in terms of how things get done. As with the timing of the laundry, one must plan errands according to the pace of life in this town.

As we step outside, our next door neighbor Giuseppina greets us — she likes to pop open her window shutters and sing, *"Cucu!"* as if she were the bird in a clock. As today is a bit cool — 19° C, or about 66° F, which in her estimation is practically Arctic — she expresses concern that we're terribly underdressed, without even a scarf. We assure her we're fine, and we try to impart that we especially welcome the crispness after the long and hot summer we had all endured. Giuseppina reluctantly accepts our reasoning, but still shivers at the sight of our slightly exposed necks.

A 10-minute stroll through the cobbled streets leads us to Soriano's bustling *piazza*. A quick stop in the *macelleria* (butcher) and the *fruttivendolo* (produce shop) yields some of our groceries for our next few meals. The ever-smiling Matteo greets us — *"Ciao, cari"* — as he loads up his little work truck with produce to deliver around town. He likes that I'm also called Matteo by many of our neighbors, and he's always happy to advise us on seasonal items — what they are, where they're from, how to prepare them.

With our grocery bags filled, we head down the hill to Bar La Luigina, where we sit on the patio overlooking the valley (and our house!). We're meeting our dear friend Floriana to discuss our upcoming concert together. Though she's Italian, she's fluent in English — a Cambridge-certified instructor, in fact. She sometimes indulges us in our efforts to practice our Italian. In return, we offer her a few "choice" colloquialisms in English that may not have made it into her standard curriculum. (Then again, sometimes she surprises us with phrases like "okey-dokey.")

Just as we've sufficiently covered the business at hand, the town's siren howls again — it's much louder here, in the middle of town. We shift this business meeting into social mode, and we switch from *caffè* to *aperitivi*. These cocktails come, as always, with an assortment of munchies — potato chips, peanuts, maybe some olives and crunchy bread. As we eat and drink, we watch the people coming and going — chatting with one another, walking their dogs, tending to their shops and their daily business. We feel simultaneously at home and profoundly foreign. Again we remark to ourselves, "I can't believe we live here."

Later in the afternoon we're back at our apartment, tying up a few loose ends of work. We hear a familiar voice at our front window, softly calling: *"Matteo... Matteo..."* Pietro always calls us to the door this way — he never knocks or rings the bell.

I check for Hoover. He's at the other end of the house, catatonic on the couch, so I feel safe opening the door. Pietro is Giuseppina's dad, and he built this house some 60 years ago. He has a small crate in his arms: a half-dozen eggs in a bowl, fresh from the chickens' "back-sides," a sack full of chestnuts, and a big *zucca* — what we'd call a butternut squash. *"Ciao Matteo... Ecc' dal orto mio."* — Here, this is from my garden. Pietro speaks no English, only Sorianese (the local Italian dialect), so communication with us is always a bit uncertain, but there's no doubting his generous desire that we enjoy sharing in his bounty. He tries to explain to us a few ways we could prepare these foodstuffs, lest we mistreat his produce.

When he assesses — probably accurately — that we won't understand any more than what he's already told us, Pietro bids us *"Buona serata e buon appetito!"*

Just then Hoover comes bolting out — he has roused himself from his torpor to sprint to the front of the house, taking advantage of my lapse in door protocols. He takes four or five steps outside and... immediately flops to the ground at Pietro's feet. As he rolls in the driveway, he morphs almost instantly from white to ashtray-colored. Pietro raises a bemused eyebrow and regards Hoover curiously, muttering something about a *"miccione sporco"* ("big dirty kitten") before shuffling off to his place next door, his hoarse chuckle lingering behind him.

After retrieving and brushing off Hoover, we get to work preparing our dinner. As we dodge each other in our tiny kitchen, we remark to each other yet again — as we do frequently — how grateful we are for the highly unlikely circumstances that led us to this point. Because here we are, a couple of American symphony musicians who quit our jobs, sold nearly everything, moved into a tiny apartment in a picture-perfect Italian hill town, working as performers, writers, and travel advisors, and enjoying this life in Italy — cats and neighbors and sirens and church bells and all.

This is the story of those circumstances — and of what we did to make it all happen.

CHAPTER 2
The Big Idea

NOVEMBER 2018

O UR FRIENDS BO AND LEE came to our place for dinner one night for a three-course spread inspired by our travels to Italy. We'd gotten to know them as fellow Italophiles in Nashville, so we wanted share some of the goodies we'd brought back to the US from a recent trip to Italy: *pecorino* cheese and jams, white *zolfini* beans, and a sampling of *digestivo* liqueurs, as well as recipes inspired by dishes — *peposo* (Tuscan beef stew) and hand-rolled *pici* pasta — that we had enjoyed in restaurants on our travels. We liked to bring back a bit of Italy to the States whenever we could, aiming to relive the experience of traveling there.

"You guys have such a connection to Italy," Lee observed. "You should just live there!"

Of course we agreed. The idea had been a longstanding dream of ours, ever since we first visited Italy on our honeymoon in 2006. In the following years we were drawn back again and again — the food, the culture and history, and the rhythm of everyday life in the "real Italy" we'd experienced by always visiting small towns, on some 40 trips. With our three jobs in the music business in Nashville, we felt like we were constantly on the go from one project to the next. The Italian lifestyle appealed to us: taking time to enjoy family, friends, and food, just like we were doing this evening.

Bo and Lee started telling us about a town they had visited a couple of times. "You really must go to Soriano, it's just the most perfect, charming little town." Over and over again during our multi-hour dinner, they returned to the topic, describing the town, showing us pictures, relaying stories, all in an excited and giddy tone. They displayed a level of fervor that would shame a Boston Red Sox fan during the playoffs.

We regarded their enthusiasm with a bit of skepticism. After several years advising travelers in our Little Roads Europe business, we had heard this many times before: The one little Italian town that someone had visited (or whose cousin or friend or veterinarian said they had visited) is always the most beautiful, idyllic place. The thing is, there are hundreds, maybe thousands, of charming little Italian towns. Over the years we have made a point of visiting a great many of them! So the idea that someone had found "the perfect town" was nothing new to our ears.

But we trusted these friends, as we seemed to have a lot in common where Italy was concerned, and a few things stood out to us in their description of the place. First, the town seemed to draw very few American tourists — always a selling point for us. Second, during one of their short stays there, Bo had been invited to march in medieval garb as part of one of the neighborhoods during the annual Chestnut Festival, a weeks-long event. An Italian village that would so readily welcome a foreigner was remarkable, in our view.

"And the real estate there is really inexpensive, too," Lee added. "We're in the process of buying an apartment in the historic center for about 50 thousand bucks, and some places are a lot less than that."

On every trip to Italy over the years, we'd always take a few moments to stare, starry-eyed, at the houses listed in the windows of *immobiliare* (real estate) offices, in southern Tuscany in particular. But the high costs made the idea seem nothing more than a pipe dream. After all, we were classical musicians in the orchestral business. We played recording sessions when the work became available, and we had a "side hustle" creating itineraries for travelers to Italy and Ireland. We were not exactly what most people would call "rich," so the idea of buying an apartment in Italy — even for less than 50 grand — seemed impossible.

We did manage to travel to Europe three or four times a year, but that was only possible because the rest of the time we were consummate cheapskates. We wore the same clothes for years. We had just one car, bought used. We seldom dined out, and never spent money on fancy coffee drinks or avocado toast. Come winter, we'd hold off on turning the heat on at least until Thanksgiving, and in the summer we didn't turn the AC on until July 4. Zeneba's colleagues in the violin section would occasionally hold "Fancy Shoe Night," but she could never participate because she had worn the same pair of black pumps for every concert for at least a decade. And my "hairstyling" was (and still is) done on our porch with a pet-hair trimmer. Our colleagues — who made the same money as we did, as we were all under a union contract with the orchestra — thought we were crazy slobs. (They were half right.) Spending your discretionary money on experiences instead of objects has gotten a lot more popular now, but 10 years ago it still struck people as a little strange.

We saved everything we could for trips overseas. Our schedule was hectic — sometimes four different concerts a week just with the orchestra, on top of organizing our chamber ensemble concerts and taking recording work when it arose.

We didn't like that the expected — and respected — response to the question "How are you?" in the US was always "I'm really busy." But we were.

Managing our schedules was a monumental task — Zen called it the "burning Jenga puzzle." Nevertheless, she made sure we carved out a week here and a week there, to take a trip and explore some small corner in Europe. Sometimes Ireland, sometimes England or Germany, and even Belgium one time.

But again and again we kept returning to Italy. Something about it just seemed "right" for us. We certainly felt like we fit in better with the people there than we did with our neighbors in the US. The sense that Italy is part of a larger global community; the sense of safety we feel in a place where guns aren't commonplace; the care for the environment; the value placed on good health and food practices — these elements of life seemed to align with what's important to us.

And, of course, we loved Italy's food culture, which was why we brought it home to share with friends whenever we could. As we toasted one another's health with an herbal *amaro* we had brought back from a remote town in western Tuscany, we decided that we'd take Lee and Bo's advice and spend a week exploring Soriano. Maybe we'd even look at some properties.

Conveniently, we had already planned a trip to Italy for the following February. We had been assigned to write an article for a travel magazine about visiting Italy on a budget, and we had already booked our flights and a rental car for a total of $1,100 — a good start to an inexpensive trip. A visit to Soriano would fit in nicely. It would be out of the way and, therefore, less expensive than the hot spots, but beautiful and charming. At least, we hoped so!

FEBRUARY 2019

On its face, there was nothing unusual about this trip. We had done this dozens of times over the years. The only difference was the region — northern Lazio, which we usually would pass through on the way to Toscana or points farther north.

We had booked a little apartment for the week, directly above Soriano's central *piazza,* for €280. We flew into Rome's airport, picked up our car, and set off to see the town for ourselves.

The town is properly called Soriano nel Cimino, as it sits low on the shoulders of the Cimino mountains, part of the pre-Apennine range. It's dominated by a 13th-century castle of the Orsini, a highly influential and powerful family dynasty in medieval times. Approaching from the coast, we watched first the mountain and then the castle itself looming ever closer.

As we drove up toward the center of town, we took a few

hairpin curves and headed up a narrow one-way street: Shops lined one side — bakery, fruit shop, butcher, cheese-monger, another bakery, another fruit shop — while on the other side a little public park overlooked over a small valley. We could see a woodsy hillside, dotted with a few colorful houses and small apartment buildings. A handful of sheep and goats grazed on a steep grassy slope next to a small olive and fruit grove.

But we couldn't focus on that vista at the moment: The narrow street was bustling, with shoppers constantly darting across the road, heedless of traffic, ducking in and out of the shops to get their bread, meat, cheese, and whatever else they needed — it was nearing lunchtime. We drove up the street at a snail's pace. While it's technically a street for driving, the walkers definitely control the field.

The tight one-way pattern gave way to a chaotic flow of cars and pedestrians as it opened up into the *piazza*. A giant cathedral dominated one end, and next to it a medieval gate led up to the *Rocca* — the castle section of the town. We parked in front of the cathedral — something we'd never have done in years past, lest we run afoul of traffic restrictions. But in this case the signage was in our favor, so we grabbed a space and got out of the car.

People seemed to swirl around us, going about their business. A pharmacy, a hardware store, a bank, two tobacco shops, two restaurants, a half-dozen other stores, and, most importantly, not two but *three* bars — were all within a stone's throw of one another. This was the heart of the town.

We were immediately struck, in all of this hubbub, by the lack of touristy trappings: No tour buses, no signage in multiple languages, and no English. All around us we heard only the singsong of spoken Italian that we've come to love so much. (Though here it was mixed with ... something else, which made it hard for us to catch everything being said around us.)

This was a town for its citizens, first and foremost. A real town for real people.

We found the door to the apartment we were renting for the week, and we sent a WhatsApp to our host: *"Siamo arrivati!"* — We've arrived!

She responded right away. "Look for my father Luciano, he's waiting in the *piazza*. He'll let you in and show you around. About 60, tall, skinny, white hair."

We looked around. There were about a dozen guys who fit that description, chatting in several different little groups — outside the bar, in front of the cathedral, by the *tabaccheria*, outside the other bar. We approached one group to ask a couple of likely suspects if one of them was Luciano.

Just then a deafening siren washed over the piazza, rising to a high pitch then falling gradually. It was exactly like the tornado siren that we'd occasionally hear in Tennessee, but this one was mounted on a clock tower just steps away. We glanced nervously at the other people in the square, but no one flinched. Pedestrians crossing the street continued on their way. Those who were talking, suspended their conversation for a moment while the siren wailed. And just as the siren reduced to a manageable volume, the church bells began chiming — a prettier sound, but still really loud, as we were directly under them.

A minute later the bells finished their tune, and people resumed their conversations. Thus were we introduced to Soriano's siren — once a WWII air-raid warning, later a work signal, and now a thrice-daily timekeeper and reminder of Soriano's history. It sounds every day at 8 am (start of work), noon (lunch break), and 5 pm (end of work).

Over the next few minutes we failed to find Luciano, until a man matching his description came out of the apartment with another man and woman. The two turned out to be Americans also. Ten minutes earlier, Luciano had heard them speaking in the square and assumed they must be his American guests, so he had beckoned them to follow him, and they amiably complied. So he took them up the two stories for a tour of the apartment.

After they had seen the place in great detail, the couple asked him (in English), "Well, this is nice, but why are we here?" Luciano didn't speak English, but he grasped the confusion, realized his error, and brought them back out to the square. When we approached the three of them outside the door, we realized this must be the guy. *"Eccoci,"* we said, *"gli americani per l'appartamento!"* — Here we are!

We had a good laugh with the Americans — "We've seen the whole place, you'll love it!" — and they said goodbye to Luciano as if they were old friends.

This experience demonstrated a couple of things about this town: One, that so few Americans come here that Luciano figured those two talking in the *piazza* must have been his guests; and two, that the people here (if Luciano was anything to go by) are friendly, and they're also not weary of tourists. All good signs, we thought.

The apartment had a back balcony that overlooked that same valley we had seen as we drove up the hill into town, and a big front window that looked directly out to the *piazza*, across from the cathedral and above all the bustle. Altogether, it was a prime position for people-watching and exploring this hopping little town.

We had organized an appointment mid-week to meet Marco, the real estate manager Lee and Bo had worked with. During the intervening days, we explored the region. We saw olive and nut groves, vineyards on lake-side hills, wide open farms, and forested mountains. There were also ruins of Roman towns and outposts; an ancient road lined with Etruscan caves guarded by wild donkeys; a forest full of massive 16th-century sculptures of monsters; a *palazzo* with an elaborate Renaissance fountain spread over several acres; and dozens of fascinating little medieval towns and castles, any number of which could have been "the" perfect Italian town.

And we found much to explore in Soriano itself: The fantastical fountain statuary in its 16th-century palace; the Faggeta, a dense UNESCO forest of beech and chestnut on the Cimino mountain above the town; and, of course, the medieval Orsini castle that crowns the hillside and overlooks the town. As musicians, we took it as a special sign that one of the castle rooms is a museum installation featuring about 30 working gramophones, pianolas, and wax cylinder players from the 19th century. It was a singular experience for us, listening to a wax recording of Italian opera on an antique player in a medieval Italian castle.

We found it invigorating, moving in the midst of the daily life in Soriano. Our stay happened to coincide with a street festival one night, complete with parades of costumed groups presenting choreographed walks across the town square. But even on non-festival days, the square buzzed with activity. Walking or driving through the *piazza* seemed like a contact sport.

One late afternoon, we sat with a couple of glasses of wine at our window and watched a "drama" unfold in the square below. Several drivers had parked haphazardly, and some were blocked in. A bit of horn-honking ensued, followed by several people hustling in and out of the bar and the pharmacy and the hardware store to discuss which car was whose, and who should move what, and when. The conversations were loud and energetic, but never angry. Eventually one driver whose car was blocked in decided there had been enough discussion. He got in his car and proceeded to skillfully maneuver out of the space past the others. It was something like a 10-point turn, his little Fiat 500 demonstrating the benefits of a small car in a small town. Eventually things got sorted out, and everyone proceeded with their evenings.

Halfway through the week, we went to our appointment with Marco. He speaks almost no English, and while our Italian was functional as travelers, we were still pretty primitive when it came to talking about things like plumbing, electric outlets, and other basic homeowner vocabulary. So we engaged Hamish, an Australian whose family had lived in Soriano for 10 years running an English-language school for Italians. Hamish and his little brother had been steeped in the language and culture since childhood, so they're fully bilingual.

Marco and Hamish took several hours to walk us around the town, showing us about a dozen properties. Throughout, Hamish helped us discuss specifics with Marco, but the excursion became an ad hoc Italian lesson as well. We did manage to catch some of what Marco told us in Italian about each place — certainly the price (we know our numbers!), and some of the discussion of the age or condition of various elements — the sink, the gas supply, the window, the roof. And we learned two key phrases that applied to everything: *"Tutto incluso?"* ("Everything is included in the price?" The answer varied depending on the property.) And *"trattabile"* — negotiable. The latter was key, of course.

We had always liked the idea of living within the old medieval fortifications of one of these old towns — an idea formed from many visits over many years to similar places. So we began looking at apartments in the "Rocca," the oldest quarter of town, which surrounds the castle. Walking through the old fortress gate, we came to Gigi's Pizzeria, a spot that Bo and Lee had mentioned to us as their favorite hangout. Smelling what they were cooking and watching the gaggle of locals snacking and chatting at the outside tables, it was easy to see why.

But we were on a mission, so after Marco and Hamish greeted a few friends, we proceeded up into the Rocca, a fascinating maze of tiny winding streets, picturesque doors, ancient stone structures — it seemed like a movie set from a medieval period piece. The interior of one house we viewed was just rough stone on one side — a wall shared with the castle itself! Some homes were more or less ready to move in. Others needed various levels of repair or restoration.

As evocative and interesting as this area was, we became daunted at the prospect of such narrow streets, all the steps, and the small windows (therefore, not much natural light) in many of these medieval buildings. Certainly, some of our hesitation came from the fact that we were both huffing and puffing behind spry Marco and youthful Hamish, arriving at each apartment a breathless, sweaty mess. We missed much of what Marco said as we both tried discreetly to catch our breath and pretend we weren't sweating through our clothing. Attempting to look cool and reserved took all of our effort. But I guess we weren't as slick as we thought we were, because Marco saw through our expert thespianship and asked if we needed a rest. "Could we take a look at some apartments that have ground-floor access?" I asked, trying to stand up straight and look athletic.

"Va bene," Marco assured us. He had some places to show us in other parts of town.

We walked through the old cobbled streets, up and down stone steps. Even outside of the castle area, everything felt ancient. Strolling along Via 5 Giugno (June 5th Street), we took a stairway between houses, worn down by centuries of foot treads. We asked Marco about one of the street signs — Via Ospedale Vecchio. Yes, he explained, and pointed — that building there, it was the old hospital, many years ago. Zeneba quipped that she might need to visit the hospital if she didn't watch her footing on these steps. Hamish translated this for Marco, who chuckled and nodded. *"Vero, vero, attenzione,"* he said — True, true, watch yourself.

The winding streets led us to the area opposite the castle, on the other side of the valley. This was sometimes called the "Castagni" neighborhood, after a particular row of chestnut trees, and for its position on the road leading up to the mountain forest.

Below Via dei Castagni was a little one-way street. We walked down a short driveway to a wooden door, and entered a narrow white building attached to a huge gray house.

"This one is 50 square meters, built about 50 years ago," Marco said. About 530 square feet, it included the ground floor and an upstairs attic. And the price was 26 thousand — less than a new car in the US.

The apartment was small, and a bit cramped and dark: A little foyer/kitchen led to a short, narrow "hallway." To one side, a tiny bedroom space was walled off. The bedroom door didn't open all the way because it bumped into the bed. We imagined you'd have to fling yourself from the "hallway" into the bed, but you'd have to watch out for the big clunky wardrobe that was also stuffed in there. It looked as if the owner had assembled the bed and wardrobe first, then built the flimsy wall around them. On the other side of the hallway, a sliding pocket door led to a pocket-sized bathroom, large enough for only one person at a time, and only if that person exercised caution and made no sudden movements.

The hallway led to a small living room — we had to duck our heads a bit to avoid the wood-and-iron stairway that led, awkwardly, to a low, roof-beamed attic space. Upstairs we could see two single beds in the middle of what could have been a used-furniture store. In fact, the whole apartment was stuffed with the owner's furniture, and a plethora of other belongings.

"Tutto incluso," Marco said, grinning. I saw Zen giving the stink-eye to a huge gold-framed velvet painting and several cardboard boxes of random junk, and I knew she was wondering if napalm was legal here. The living room was lit by a single bare bulb hanging from the ceiling. We wondered when the police interrogation would begin. It was not what we might have imagined for a romantic Italian pied-à-terre.

But as we looked around at all the grim clutter, Marco raised the metal shutters on the door at the other end of the place. Light flooded into the apartment.

"Venite, guarda qui," he said, still smiling — Come, look here...

We stepped through the doors... and the view took our breath away.

We found ourselves on a covered terrace on the corner of the building, looking straight across at the imposing castle, perched above a colorful stack of houses with nothing but blue sky behind it. Below and to the right were an olive grove and a grassy hillside where sheep and goats grazed peacefully. And beyond that, we took in a hundred miles of landscape — the vast Valle Tevere (Tiber River) and the hills of the Colle Sabine, with the Monti Appennini, many of the peaks still snow-capped, looming in the distance.

We looked at a few more places that day before Marco and Hamish left us alone to talk about everything over a *prosecco* and a piece of pizza at Gigi's. Later that afternoon we asked Marco if we could go back and look at that little terrace house again. And the next day, we told him we wanted to buy it.

He was surprised at how fast we made this decision and how quickly we acted on it. We were too, but we also knew from experience that sometimes you need to force yourself to do something good for yourself by taking a big step, like signing up for a marathon, or making a colonoscopy appointment. (We hoped this process would be more like the former and less like the latter.)

Like many businesses in Italy, real estate deals work differently than they do in the States. The American sense of urgency and immediate action is just not the Italian way. It's not uncommon for a property to sit on the market for years, and once it does sell, the wheels turn slowly. We understood that the sale wouldn't be finalized for weeks, perhaps months. The owner's family lived in Austria, so communications and document signing would be a slow process.

Knowing we were only in the country for a couple more days, Marco arranged for us to meet with Gabriele, a *muratore* (contractor). Gabriele walked through the apartment and, again with the help of Hamish's translating skills, we discussed a few items we already knew needed work — a minor roof repair; a new railing for the terrace; removing one of the bedroom walls; and a half-dozen other little things. Gabriele would e-mail us an estimate for the work, which he could start once we finalized the purchase. We also talked with Marco about arranging for someone to take away most of the stuff that had been left by the previous owner — at least a couple of pickup truck loads, we guessed.

Later we sat in Marco's office, which was strewn with reams of paperwork from a dozen different deals he was working on at the time. He explained to us that there remained one more point we had to address, before Gabriele could do any work: He would need power and water to be hooked up to the house. Electric was no problem, but Marco needed another deposit to set up the water service, and it would be easiest if we had cash — 140 euro should do it, he explained (in Italian). We handed it over to him, seven €20 notes. He folded them in half and clipped the wad to our folder full of papers with a sticky note that read: *"Servizio idrico Matt e Zen."*

"A posto," he said — Everything is sorted. Despite the apparent chaos of paperwork in front of us (only one folder of which had anything to do with us), there was something inherently reassuring in Marco's manner. It all felt like a huge amount of trust, to hand over so much control (and a lot of money!) to make this transaction work. But we looked at it all as the price of admission, and we felt comfortable leaving it to Marco's expertise to manage the details. Something about him seemed so trustworthy; his demeanor overcame our big-city cynicism.

As he walked us to the front door, and I could see in Zen's face that she was wrestling with a range of emotions and holding back tears. We just bought a house in Italy!

"Grazie mille Marco" she stammered. *"Tu sei fare il nostro sogni essere vero,"* which means something like "You are to make the our dreams to be true." But he understood what she meant. Instead of the typical Italian double face-kiss, she gripped him

in a big American-style hug. He stood immobilized, bewildered at the outpour of emotion.

On one hand, it seemed a crazy, impulsive thing to do. But it had indeed been a dream for such a long time, so it really seemed right. It occurred to us that, despite its small size, having this apartment would give us a perfect "base" for multiple trips to explore the region — the northern half of Lazio (excluding Rome) would be an excellent subject for our next Little Roads guidebook. Not to mention the appeal of sitting on that terrace with a coffee in the morning and an *aperitivo* in the evening.

The idea that it might be something more — that it might be a permanent home — didn't start to form for a few more months.

CHAPTER 3
Lawyers and Bankers and Builders ... *O Dio!*

APRIL 2019

*M*ORE OR LESS AS SOON AS we returned home from our February trip, Zen had an idea, which she conveniently shared with me in the middle of the night.

"I think we should talk to an immigration lawyer," she said, her voice jolting me awake in the dark at 3 am.

The idea (she explained, once my heart rate had returned to something like normal) was just to learn about what *could* happen — what we would need to do to work in Italy, or perhaps to retire early there. At the very least, we could have somebody authoritative tell us we had no chance, so we could quit fooling ourselves.

As a married couple with jobs in the same symphony orchestra, we considered ourselves privileged. Such a job setup is a rarity in our business. Nevertheless, in recent years we had both been feeling that we were ready for something different. And we both wanted to exit our careers at a stage when people would still ask "Why are you leaving?" not "*When* are you leaving?"

Of course this was easier said than done. Most classical musicians, especially orchestra musicians, are not wealthy people. It's a modest living. In this business, retirement tends to come late, if ever.

We had already done countless hours of reading on our own about various options for living full-time in Italy, and it was discouraging. Work visas were available for brain surgeons and rocket scientists, not for musicians or people with a side-hustle creating itineraries for tourists. A retirement visa seemed more likely, but not anytime soon. If we lived really frugally, we could *maybe* make that happen in five or 10 years. If we wanted to move sooner, we thought, we'd need some help.

After weeks of dogged and exhaustive research, Zeneba came up with a name of an *avvocato* in Florence whose practice specialized in navigating the choppy waters of immigration into Italy. He appeared to be an out-of-the-box thinker, somebody who might be creative about how to make our idea happen.

We set up an appointment to consult with this lawyer, with lower than low expectations. We assumed he'd say "Forget it," followed by "Let's call that an hour... that'll be 240 euro, *per favore.*"

At this point we already had a trip to Italy scheduled for April. The symphony set and controlled our work schedules far in advance, and we built our own travel planning around that. We had worked out a short period of time off, which meant we'd have a tougher schedule for the rest of the season. Not only was the orchestra work incessant, but we had also started accepting every other possible freelance recording session and side gig to balance out our sudden spending for the new apartment. Other than this trip in April, we were working seven days a week from March until the end of summer.

Our plan had been to use that trip to do some travel research and gather information for a second edition of our small-town guidebook to Tuscany. But given the crazy thing we had done in February, we decided we'd better spend some time in Soriano to finish the house purchase and get the place organized. So why not also squeeze in a visit to Firenze to meet with this immigration lawyer? It seemed audacious, but again it just felt like the right step to take in this series of events.

April arrived, and we stepped off the plane in Rome with a different mood and different goals compared to our previous trips to Italy. Yes, we would still be ingesting copious amounts of wine and cheese and staying in 500-year-old buildings, but this time we were taking baby steps toward the notion of actually living here. Buying the apartment had been the first step; this *avvocato* meeting was the next.

After a few days of visiting some little towns in Tuscany, we showed up in the "big city" of Firenze. Over the years, we have built an entire travel philosophy (and business) around *not* visiting such large and heavily touristed places. Though it's generally regarded as "small" — much smaller than Nashville, and dwarfed by the likes of Rome or New York — we find the sheer size and grandeur of Firenze incredible but overwhelming.

Every step we took that day is now etched in our minds. Though just a block away from the Duomo, our guy's law offices were in a cluster of professional businesses — banks, real estate brokers, insurance companies, accounting firms, and government offices — not a spot frequented by tourists. We walked up to the big front door and rang the bell, and the receptionist buzzed us in. It was a 250-year-old building — relatively new for Firenze. We climbed the three stories to his floor, and stepped into his office. It was an old, classic lawyerly interior, with fancy antique furniture and people in impossibly cool business suits with shoes that were shiny, not scuffed-up slip-on Skechers like mine.

We felt out of place in our usual dumpy clothing.

"Well, just ask yourself if any of these guys go to work regularly in a white tie and tailcoat?" Zen tried to reassure me.

"I'm sure they'd be impressed by our black concert clothes with the white-cat-hair accents," I shot back with a grin...

But this wasn't really helping to set either of us at ease in this unfamiliar environment.

The *avvocato* was perfectly amiable, listening patiently as we explained that we'd like to move to Italy to work, or at least to retire here someday: Buying the little house, planning to write our next guidebook, and so on. We thought our travel books and our business of making itineraries might be of interest to the Italian government. We'd love to be able to live here and do that sort of work, which theoretically would be good for Italian businesses and individuals.

Through all this, the *avvocato* smiled and nodded.

Then he leaned back. His fancy leather chair made that fancy leather chair sound.

"Okay," he said. "Nobody will care about the travel stuff. The thing you two have that is compelling is your background as musicians." He flipped through the papers on his desk — the materials we had sent him ahead of time so he'd know something about us. "Twenty years in that orchestra, this long list of impressive people you've performed with, the CDs you produced, Grammy nominations, directors of your chamber ensemble, and so on."

The upshot was, we could request work visas to be concert performers and organizers of cultural events. We explained that we had been thinking about doing less music, not more. In fact, we wanted to gradually get *out* of the music business, to start doing more of our travel consulting work.

"You can still keep doing that, too," he explained. "But this is how we get you in here — as experts in music."

Zen and I were looking at each other, thinking about this idea, when he added, "And you should do it now. Not in a few years, not next year. *Now.*"

The word just hung there in the air. So did our jaws.

He explained: The Italian government had recently released their work visa quotas for that year, and among the categories they were accepting were a few of these cultural/arts visas. The *avvocato*'s help with the work visa application would not be cheap — a package price of some 4,000 euros. On the other hand, he had a perfect record: Every application he had ever filed had received approval from the government.

We took a deep breath and told him we'd discuss it. We calmly thanked him, casually handed over his fee for the hour, and coolly walked out of the offices, down the stairs and out to the street. Once we had gone a block or so, that facade of calm, cool casualness evaporated and we proceeded to lose our shit.

It sounded too good to be true. We knew it was a long-shot. We knew it would take an as-yet-inconceivable amount of logistical work and an even greater amount of luck.

We were overcome by sensory overload as we walked out of the lawyer's office onto the streets of Firenze. The famous Duomo a block away; gaggles of tourists; sharp-dressed Italian men and women darting between businesses; the aroma of espresso and colognes. We were agitated — a combination of excitement and trepidation — and we needed a quiet place to sit and talk about the options that had just been revealed to us. But this major metropolitan street in a highly touristy area wasn't it.

Despite the chaos, both on the street and in our minds, we stopped on the sidewalk and looked at each other.

"What the hell," Zen said. "Let's do it."

"Okay," I answered. "Let's give it a shot, at least."

"LET'S DO IT!" she repeated at the top of her voice, clapping her hands with joy like a little kid.

That was the moment we decided to leave the US.

Seven months later, we started a new life in Italy.

Deciding to apply for a work visa immediately changed our outlook altogether. This apartment we were buying was no longer a little getaway for us to use as a base for exploring Lazio. It was now a potential home, to which we would actually move in the imminent future.

One of the requirements for a work visa is having a place to live. Another was that we would be required to move to Italy within 90 days of approval. This would mean quitting our jobs, selling nearly everything we own, packing up what was left — including four cats! — and actually moving to live in Italy, all within about six months of the moment we left that law office.

The cats were an especially difficult and daunting question. We love our animals, and we would never think of moving and leaving them behind. From what we had already researched, the logistics and legalities involved in moving cats on an overseas flight to a foreign country would be a challenge. It would be easier to get authorization to broadcast a live Facebook video from Area 51.

And our oldest cat at the time, Mr. Weasely, had a long and varied history of expensive medical problems. Would we be able to get him the care he needed? The right food? The right medicine? The money-hemorrhaging array of doctors and specialists he might require? Weasel was a special cat. Whenever one of us was depressed or feeling ill, he'd sense our distress and lie with us for hours or days until we felt better. Over the years we had spent an eye-watering amount of money on keeping him in good health, to the point where we referred to him as "Mr. Wea$ely" in print. And he was just one of our cats; if we got these visas, we'd have to figure out how to get all four of them over to Italy with us.

We'd also have to keep this plan — even the potential of it — a secret from our colleagues and employers, at least for the time being. The classical music world tends to be strange and insular. Perhaps because of the single-minded devotion, from a young age, that's required to succeed in the business, many classical musicians regard any activity outside of their immediate field as a distraction, an aberration, a sign that one doesn't take "the art" sufficiently seriously. In our case, some of our fellow symphony musicians were already raising eyebrows at the fact that we traveled to Europe multiple times a year, resulting in the creation of a whole other not-classical-music-related business. We always felt the opposite: Our co-workers who we felt were the most interesting and well-balanced were the ones who weren't defined only by their instruments: brewers, scientists, beekeepers, mechanics, woodworkers.

Moreover, classical players do not, in general, quit orchestra jobs. The prevailing mindset is that you hold your job as long as you can hold your instrument. [An old industry joke: What's the difference between a cello and a coffin? The cadaver is on the *inside* of the coffin.] Some of our colleagues already regarded our expansion into travel planning and writing as a sign that we lacked commitment to our orchestra work. The idea that somebody might consider quitting their symphony job when barely in their 50s was practically inconceivable.

We couldn't keep it a secret forever — certainly once we put our house on the market, the cats would be out of the bag (so to speak) — but at this point, it still seemed a distant and unlikely option, and not one that our employer or our colleagues needed to hear about yet.

All of these ramifications — the jobs, the cats, selling the house, the move itself — swirled in our heads as we talked things through. But the most immediate concern for this visa application was the requirement of having a place to live. So we had to head back to Soriano to get the apartment purchase in order.

For the following week, we had taken a vacation rental place in a little village about five minutes from Soriano's *centro*. It was an apartment, one half of a house; on the adjacent side were the owners and their two little dogs. Living in a place like this felt like a taste of real life in the small town: Cooking, chatting with neighbors, watching Italian TV. (You haven't seen *CHiPs* or *The Dukes of Hazzard* until you've watched them dubbed into Italian.) It was a huge contrast to the crowds and cacophony of Firenze — quiet, peaceful, relaxing.

At least, it *could* have been relaxing if we hadn't needed to stuff every day full of busywork errands. One of the big tasks at hand was setting up a bank account, from which our various payments (utilities, taxes) could be made. Marco was kind enough to come with us to our initial meeting at the bank in the *piazza*, to explain our situation and our needs. He would have stayed there with us the entire time, we think, but we had a hunch that it would take a while, so we suggested that he move on with his day and we'd connect with him later.

Little did we know that this was going to be a many-hours, multiple-day process.

This bank is not like those in the US. The entrance is a single-person security pod: Walk up and press a button and an outer door opens. Step inside the pod, and that door closes and an interior door opens. This is a security measure we'd expect to see in *Get Smart* (which, by the way, is also fun to watch dubbed into Italian), not a small-town bank branch.

Inside, there are no comfy chairs and couches, no complimentary coffee, no rope-lines to manage whose turn it is. Waiting in line isn't really a thing here. Instead, the waiting customers are chatting with one another in a clump. Each new arrival walks up to the group of waiting customers and asks, *"Chi è l'ultima?"* — Who is the last person? Everyone knows who immediately precedes them. What at first seemed like confusion was just casualness. Everyone knows who they'll be following, and everyone cooperates.

By the time it was our turn to step up to the *consulente* desk, we were feeling pretty out of place, and definitely foreign. The advisor was extremely kind, and when we apologized in advance for speaking Italian like 5-year-old kids, she shrugged it off: *"Piano piano."* — Slowly but surely. This became a frequent refrain.

We had a folder full of every possible document we might need for such a process: Passports, drivers licenses, social security cards, birth certificates, marriage certificate — you name it, we had it with us. But despite what we thought was a high degree of preparedness, the process moved slowly. Part of it was the foreign-sounding names and places in our details. Just as Americans don't really know how to spell "Siena" or that Firenze and Florence are the same city, our *consulente* didn't catch how to spell "Walker" or "Schenectady" at a first hearing, or to know that Nashville is a city in Tennessee and not the other way around.

A larger problem was simple computer formatting: The Italian systems didn't account for the different methods of writing addresses, so there were not one-to-one correlations for city-county-state-country data fields. Our advisor struggled with how to enter birthplaces and current addresses, and how to account for our US address compared to what would be our local Soriano address — a property which we didn't yet officially own.

The *consultente* had to stop several times to consult with the bank manager. They had many rapid and complex discussions on how to enter the information and account for the discrepancies in the systems. And they had several questions for us. We only hoped we had answered usefully, and we apologized repeatedly for our limited speaking skills.

"Tranquillo; piano piano," they'd say, smiling, before resuming their decidedly not-tranquil discussion of our situation.

Ultimately, they concluded that we had to suspend the effort for the day. The branch had a "guy who was authorized to grant the correct approval and documentation to initiate an account for a non-Italian citizen." (*That* was one hell of a sentence to grasp in a foreign language!) Unfortunately, "the guy" had gone home for the afternoon, so we agreed to resume the effort the next day.

No problem, we said, we're happy to come back.

"Va bene, facciamo tutto, piano piano."

In any case, we had plenty of other things to attend to this week. Marco had arranged for us to walk through the apartment again, so we picked up the key from his office and walked the five minutes along the cobbles to the other side of town.

I was pleased with myself for having the foresight to bring my tape measure from home so we could take measurements and talk about how we'd set the place up. And now that we had our new "big idea" of moving here permanently, we needed to think about getting it to a point where we could actually live there, cats and all.

The previous owner's stuff was still in there, but we worked around it, knowing Marco would clear it out before we needed to do anything substantial. We could visualize things well enough as we measured wall space for pictures and such, and terrace space for patio furniture. After a few minutes, Gabriele (the *muratore*) arrived to discuss the bits of work that needed to be done — change this sink, take down that wall, fix the railing out there, and so on.

He smiled when he saw me measuring things out, and he pointed at my tape measure.

"Sono pollici," he chuckled; *"in Italia non ci servono."* — "Those are inches; we don't use those in Italy." (Italy, like most of the rest of the world, uses the metric system).

"Well, of course," I responded knowingly, while mentally face-palming myself. "But it's all I had handy." I grinned sheepishly at Zen, grateful that she held back the first 30 jokes that must have come to her mind in that moment.

The next couple of days were a blur of meetings. Marco had secured our *codice fiscale,* similar to a Social Security number, which would, in theory, expedite the process of opening our bank account. We spent several more hours at the bank over the next two days, watching the time tick away. The bank's computer still wasn't quite cooperating with our *consulente,* and our documents still didn't quite contain the specific information they needed to see.

Flop sweat, nail biting, fidgeting, muttering *"Mi dispiace"* ("I'm sorry") repeatedly.

"Non vi preoccupa, piano piano," they said — Don't worry about it.

To these Italian bankers, we probably didn't match their idea of Americans buying a place in Italy. In my faded cargo pants and dusty Skechers, I definitely didn't cut the figure of the dapper American property mogul they might have imagined. And perhaps they thought of us as a cliché. Italy is littered with the abandoned dreams of Americans wanting to live there. But we aimed always to approach the situation with an air of humility and gratitude, and never any expectation or entitlement.

Despite the challenges, the bank staff never seemed stressed or irritated, with us or with what we were doing. And it was the same thing with Marco, and with Gabriele, and with everyone else we worked with. Our house was a small purchase in the scheme of real estate transactions, and the contracting work was relatively minor, so to all of these folks, what we were doing was simply another task to complete, however long it took. For our newly hatched plan to work, all of these pieces really needed to fall into place starting immediately, and our suspense level was beginning to feel less like *Under the Tuscan Sun* and more like *Fast and Furious*. But our sense of urgency simply didn't translate to the pace of Soriano life.

After each day's meetings, we'd drag our frazzled selves back to our rental place, light a fire in the little kitchen fireplace (we were still enjoying quite cool weather, thanks to the proximity of the Cimino mountain), pour ourselves an inappropriately large glass of wine from an inappropriately large bottle, and try to relax watching cheesy game shows and old *Columbo* episodes dubbed into Italian.

Our third day of bank meetings was our last weekday in the country, so we were feeling the pressure even more as we watched the minute hand inching towards closing time.

At one point, *"Ding!"* Zen's phone chimed. She checked it and her eyes went wide. She looked over at me like she had just been told our house was on fire. She held up her phone so I could read the text she had received. It was from the airline: "Time to check into your return flight!"

This cranked up our agitation visibly, so much so that our *consulente* stopped and asked, *"Tutto a posto?"* — Everything okay?

Sure, we replied shakily. All good, fine terrific. So she resumed typing and muttering at the computer. Then she hit a key decisively. A printer in the adjacent cubicle started spewing out about a thousand pages of documents. She collected them, we spent several minutes signing half of them, and she stuffed the other half in a folder for us to keep. Then a few hundred more taps on her keyboard, and...

"Ecco... aperto!" she exclaimed. It's open!

We couldn't believe it. The level of difficulty of this task had been somewhere between threading a needle when your eyes have been dilated, and vaulting a fence using a pool noodle. It was about 10 minutes before 5 pm on a Friday. We thanked her profusely and shook everyone's hand — including, we think, some bewildered fellow customers. We gathered our reams of documents and exited the bank — one at a time through the "air lock" — and staggered into the *piazza*. We repressed the giddy urge to jump up and down. We had already presented a somewhat nutty aspect to the townspeople over the past few days. Instead, we clutched each other's hands, and through gritted teeth we whispered to each other "We have an Italian bank account!" In retrospect, we probably looked a bit nutty anyway.

"We should really do something for her," Zen suggested. "We should get her something like, I don't know, a new car?!?"

I shared her overwhelming sense of gratitude, and the enthusiasm to express it... but we only had a few minutes before the bank would be closed.

I ran through the *piazza* and ducked into a floral shop, explaining breathlessly (in my primitive Italian) that we needed a little gift to say thank you to someone. She pointed to a few things on a table, including an orchid, or...

"Si, perfetto!" I interrupted. We sorted the purchase quickly; and leaving Zen to apologize to the shopkeeper for my abruptness, I jogged with this potted orchid back to the bank. Whoever was in charge of watching people come through the security pod must have wondered what the hell I was doing, but, evidently deciding the orchid presented no threat, they buzzed me in.

I was grinning as I handed the pot to our bank advisor. *"Grazie mille, siamo molto grati, mille grazie!!"* I said again and again. The bankers were surprised at this exuberance and gratitude about a simple bank account. Again, to them it was just another day at work. They smiled and said some things to each other that I hoped were good-natured comments on our sanity. *"Scusame,"* I said, *"siamo Americani pazzi."* — Sorry, we are crazy Americans.

At that moment the five-o'clock siren wailed. Perfect timing. I said my *arrivederci*s (again) and hustled out of the bank. We were now late for another appointment: Marco had scheduled a meeting with a *notaio* — a notary who would finalize the documents for our house sale.

We speed-walked up the cobbles to the notary office, where Marco and the *notaio* were chatting while they waited for us.

We apologized for our lateness. *"Ma perchè?"* they asked — But why? It was only a few minutes after five — that's not even close to being late in Soriano. *"Piano piano."*

The four of us sat down at a big desk, chatted a bit, then got down to business. No computers this time, just paper documents — Marco had prepared everything in advance — and a lot of places to initial and sign. This *notaio* is bilingual, and she was required by law to read the entire transaction agreement to us in English so that we understood all the ramifications of the deal. We waited calmly and silently while she painstakingly read every page. We nodded in agreement after each period, hoping we were concealing our internal voices screaming: "For the love of god! Please!! Just take our money and let us live here!!!"

But finally the last document was read and signed. We thanked and paid the *notaio*, and we left with Marco.

"Facciamo una cosa di più," he said — One more thing to do.

The three of us walked back over to the apartment, where he ceremoniously removed the *Vendesi* ("For sale") sign from the front window, flashed us a big smile, and with a flourish of his hand, presented us with the key.

It was done.

CHAPTER 4

A Day in the Life in Nashville

JUNE 2019

*B*ACK HOME IN NASHVILLE, it was back to work as usual. Zen kept a detailed calendar of everything we had going on — she had to write tiny to fit everything, and in pencil to account for frequent changes.

I fired up the Moka pot on the stove. I had set it up the night before, so it was ready the second we got up. Zen dumped kibble for the cats, then pulled out a container of her homemade chili from the freezer. That would be our lunch between rehearsals. Zen planned things out so that on our occasional less-busy days we'd typically cook up big batches of stuff — chili, soups, her spicy red sauce. We'd freeze it in blocks so we could easily eat good meals on hectic days such as this one, which were more and more frequent.

Zen took Mr. Weasely into the master bedroom to give him one of his medicines, a special one that we had to mix with tuna fish to get him to eat it. While he ate in solitude, we took care of a couple of e-mails from travel clients.

Then it was off to rehearsal at the symphony hall downtown. We slung our instruments on our backs and hopped on our scooters. This was a brief fun bit — our commute to work was under two miles, but by car it could sometimes take an hour or more, depending on traffic. With our little 50cc scooters, even with a top speed of only about 27 mph, we could slip between lines of cars and dodge traffic and make great time. I drew considerable attention with my cello sitting up on the seat behind me; people passing me on the bridge often slowed down to take my picture.

We arrived, as usual, about 20 minutes before our 10 am rehearsal. As it ran under a union contract, the symphony started rehearsals at exactly 10:00:00 am. If you sat down at 10:00:01, you were late.

The relatively new multimillion-dollar symphony hall was constructed in a classic style, modeled after the Concertgebouw in Amsterdam. It was also designed to be acoustically perfect, an instrument in itself. Playing the day's program in that space — some Beethoven and Verdi — was a really fine experience, exactly what it was built for.

Zen and I would frequently exchange glances across the orchestra — we could wordlessly communicate a great deal. Today she looked particularly stressed; I assumed it was her usual discomfort with our conductor's voice. He had a very loud speaking voice in general, and he tended to bark ear-splitting, one-word instructions to the orchestra while we were playing. These had a similar timbre to an air horn at a basketball game. (They were often counterproductive as well. While we played a quiet passage of music, he'd suddenly scream *"Dolce!!!"* at the top of his lungs, yielding a result that was anything but sweet.) Zen's seat was directly in front of his podium, right in the kill zone of his air-horn voice, so she always wore an ear plug in one ear at rehearsals, taking it out only for concerts.

At our break — precisely 15 minutes, also timed to the second — I walked over to Zen to ask if she was okay. "I'm fine," she replied, "but when I was feeding Weasely today, I got tuna juice all over my dress." It had gotten baked in the summer heat on the scoot to work, too, and she didn't realize it until she sat down to play.

So she — and everyone around her — had to go through the rest of the rehearsal in that lovely warm-tuna cloud. I was lucky, as the aroma didn't reach as far as the cello section. (I did hope the "Maestro" was enjoying it, at least.)

When the digital rehearsal clock hits 12:30:00 the personnel manager always walks on stage and says "Thank you!" to dismiss us for lunch. Such is the highly regulated orchestra schedule.

Our lunch break, as always, was exactly 90 minutes. We scooted home — a nine-minute ride in this case. Since we lived so close to downtown, this was our usual routine. The ride was fun, and at home we could hang out with our cats and have a hot lunch. We also saved a lot of money by not joining our colleagues for lunch at a restaurant every work day. And at home we had the chance to get some more non-symphony work done. There was always another client question, another post to write, another bill to take care of.

"Can you heat up the chili while I get out of this damn tuna dress?" Zen asked. I was happy to oblige, of course. She changed into one of her finest all-polyester dresses.

We wolfed down our lunch and took care of some business. Then it was back on our scooters and back to the hall. It had started to get hot, and hotter still when we got downtown. At this time of day, the downtown area started to turn chaotic.

Nashville's downtown had changed a lot since we moved there in 1999. Zen and I both lived downtown when hardly anyone was there — just a barbecue place, a record shop, a guitar shop, and a few honky-tonk bars where local bands played live music. It was "Music City," and it was a real place. We used to enjoy playing an all-Mozart concert and then going out to hear live blues, country, or jazz.

But it had gradually turned into a sort of Epcot caricature of itself, a drunken frat party scene. Pedal taverns clogged the narrow streets, filled with bachelorettes or dudes drinking and singing pop tunes in between screaming *"Whooooo!"* in an effort to get passers-by to look at them. A dozen bars on a single block blasted music at ridiculous levels, creating an incomprehensible cacophony of sound. Many longtime locals derisively referred to the whole downtown mob scene as Nashville's "honky-tonk-industrial complex."

One recent development in Music City's downtown entertainment was a farm tractor pulling a flatbed trailer with a beer keg and haybales, and another towing a huge hot tub. The latter was rented out for multiple liquor-fueled sessions each day. At one point we had to pass this mobile petri dish to get around it. "If one drop of that filthy ****ing ****-filled water gets on me..." Zen said menacingly. The sentiment was clear. She didn't need to finish the sentence.

And this was just a little before 2 pm. The downtown madness would only get worse as the hours rolled on. We pulled up, slightly irritated but still on time. We walked into the hall, which now was cooled to an icy Arctic chill against the muggy heat outside. It took our instruments — and our bodies — a while to adjust to these abrupt changes.

That afternoon's rehearsal was for a different concert that week: a rock band tribute show. It was like a new stage compared to the "simple" symphonic setup from the morning's rehearsal. A 30-piece drum set was front and center, ringed with microphones and surrounded by plexiglass and foam sound barriers. A rack of guitars stood next to it, flanked by countless guitar effects pedals. A dozen wedge monitors lined the front of the stage. Thick audio and electrical cables snaked all over the stage, connecting dozens of microphones placed throughout the orchestra. The band's bass player was already onstage — he had his own amplifier, which seemed as big as our Honda. A sound guy was thumping the pedal on the bass drum, which had a fat microphone stuck right into the front. We could already tell that this was going to be a Loud Show.

Contrary to common impressions, classical musicians typically enjoy many kinds of music. I myself am a closet blues guy, and Zen is a die-hard Sinatra fan, and we both like all sorts of other stuff. But these pop concerts had become probably around 70 percent of what we played in our jobs. Moreover, the amplification was cranked up to an insane degree. Though technically our contracts had decibel limitations, these were rarely heeded. Ear plugs wouldn't cut it. To protect our hearing, Zen and I both bought the kind of protective ear coverings that landscaping guys wear. Some of our colleagues followed suit. We felt a bit strange, playing a concert looking like an airport ground crew, but the volume levels on stage at these shows were potentially damaging to our hearing to an irreparable degree. So those ear covers kept our eardrums intact.

They did nothing, however, to protect us from the low bass and drum frequencies. It was an effect similar to the approaching dinosaur making the glass of water vibrate in *Jurassic Park*. But instead of the water, it was our internal organs shaking, and instead of a Tyrannosaurus Rex, it was 1.21 gigawatts of bassosaurus and megalodrums. The effect of this was visceral, in a literal sense. (It was not uncommon for Zen to have to come off the stage at the end of these shows, head to the bathroom, and vomit — the result of her insides being severely rearranged.)

In these pops configurations, the orchestral musicians, especially the strings, were largely unheard. That was okay with us — we understood that audiences for these concerts were coming mainly to see the band. But we felt a bit irrelevant. It was not a collaborative artistic experience, and the hall's finely crafted reverberation acoustics were wasted behind a wash of amplified sound.

But that was the gig.

After that second rehearsal, we headed back out into the heat. A drunk "bro" was just zipping up his fly after peeing in the bushes next to the hall where we parked our scooters. Rush-hour traffic had set in, and the pedal taverns had already resulted in at least one unfortunate bachelorette getting sick all over the street.

We had a recording session to attend at a studio south of town at 5 pm. Despite being nimble on our scooters, the ride to the recording studio took longer than we'd have liked. Some streets were blocked off for events, others had detours to accommodate construction cranes. In these days in Nashville, a new high-rise office or apartment went up every couple of weeks.

We pulled up to the studio with 15 minutes to spare. It was a four-hour session, this time recording Christmas music for some sort of Disney movie-themed ride at a theme park in Japan. We'd record short snippets one at a time, sometimes only a few seconds. It was an engineer's job to spend hours piecing it all together afterwards. Like the symphony rehearsal, the session included breaks that were union-regulated but less strictly applied — a 10-minute break every hour. During the breaks, musicians waited in line for two bathrooms. While we stood there, we'd try to get some tidbits of work done on our phones. (Occasionally, not every musician made it to the bathroom before the break ended.)

We apparently did a good job playing that evening, recording what felt like a never-ending series of ringtones. We got all the charts "in the can" earlier than planned, so we were released a little before 9 pm. We wearily shouldered our instruments and got back on our scooters.

The ride home was nice — it was dark now, and traffic had dissipated, and so had the worst of the heat of the day. Zen even donned a long wispy scarf, which fluttered in the wind behind her like a kite as we scooted.

"Should we get some takeout?" I yelled to her as we rode side by side.

"You think we should?" Zen yelled back, her cheapskate instinct kicking in. She knew mine was just as strong. But after a moment she answered her own question. "Okay, good idea, we still have some stuff to do when we get home."

"And tomorrow we have pretty much the same schedule as today," I added. So we agreed to pick up some Thai food. I called it in at the next red light. Takeout was something we got only rarely and reluctantly. We usually considered it a thing of necessity, rather than enjoyment. Eating dinner at 10 pm was not our ideal circumstance but cooking at that hour was even less so.

Colored spotlights lit up the bridge arching across the river from downtown. From the top of the span we could see the streets and buildings of downtown splayed out, all lights and music. From up here, Nashville looked vibrant, exciting. The construction cranes were mostly invisible in the skyline silhouette. When we came down off the bridge, we could feel the air temperature drop immediately. We picked up our Thai noodles and coconut soup and green curry — we were fortunate to live in a neighborhood with a lot of good restaurants of all types — and continued on to our house.

Home at last, we opened up the windows, and the scent of our garden's roses wafted through the house with the cooler air. The cats circled us in the kitchen like sharks — they were under the impression we had been gone for a week, not a day. Zen lit a single candle, our preferred response to the stage and studio lights under which we'd been baking all day. We "dined" at the coffee table by its little flicker, dealing with a few last e-mails between bites.

For a few years now, we had been feeling like the schedules that we had been keeping had become too much for us. We had to juggle multiple jobs to maintain the creature comforts that we enjoyed, and thus we didn't have the time to enjoy them. We were aware of this contradiction, but we had never known exactly how to change it. It was a paradox.

"It feels like we work harder to afford the cost of working harder," Zen observed.

Now, though, after meeting that lawyer, and after buying that tiny apartment, we could see a glimmer of an opportunity — a possible path toward something much simpler, something that would give us more time to enjoy our lives. We could imagine ourselves drastically paring down, giving up a lot of material things — not to mention walking away from a steady income. We would try to trade all of that in exchange for time.

We wanted to buy more of our own time.

But here was yet another paradox: To buy our time in this sense, we needed to accomplish an insanely complex series of tasks, and in an extremely short time.

-

CHAPTER 5

Mission Impossible:
The *stufa* and the *nulla osta*

AUGUST 2019

*F*ILING FOR THE WORK VISA, as our *avvocato* had urged, took on a *Mission: Impossible* heist-movie kind of feel. Each task had strict time parameters and logistical restrictions that would have confounded Steven Hawking. Getting them all accomplished in tandem was like putting together a royal wedding with a week's notice.

First: the work visa. Work visa applications must be delivered in person — in our case, to the Italian Consulate in Detroit. Appointments were scarce and difficult to get, but we managed to schedule one for July, when the symphony would be on hiatus. But when our appointment rolled around, we lacked a key document, the *nulla osta*. That translates very roughly to "no problems," an indication that we had no criminal history or other problematic past, and that our application could proceed uninhibited. So we had to postpone and reschedule the Consulate appointment for September 17. This was nerve-wracking: the symphony would be in season at that time, and it was likely they would deny us the time off, and this September date was the only appointment available until November!

November was a no-go. We had been talking with a pet shipper, who informed us that only one cat could go onboard with us on the plane. The other three would have to fly in the cargo hold. Pets were not allowed in cargo below a certain temperature, so we would have to fly by mid-November at the latest. That meant we *had* to make the September date work. *If* they granted us a work visa, we had to use it within three months, or lose it — forever. So *everything* rode on us getting that *nulla osta* document so we could apply for the work visa. Then, if we were successful, we would have to uproot everything and move to Italy by mid-November.

It will come as no surprise that getting the *nulla osta* required us to pick it up in person, at a government office, in Italy. We also had to get our apartment, which was currently stuffed to the gills with the previous owner's stuff, into suitable condition, so we could move in in November — with four cats! — in hopes the whole enterprise was successful. Oh, did I mention that there was no heat in the house? So we had to figure that out, as well.

We already had tickets to Italy for August that we'd bought on sale back in 2018, intending to do research for our travel business. We scrapped that idea, and focused all our energy on accomplishing the tasks at hand, to give ourselves a chance at our dream of moving to Italy.

Banking on the hope that our scheme would work, we took a week off in early August for what we privately called a "Farewell Tour" — traversing multiple states to visit family and friends. We weren't sure if some of them could or would visit us in Italy, and we wanted to eat and drink and laugh together one more time. We didn't have much time to get emotional about it, since it was such an insane, whirlwind tour, and The Big Heist was just around the corner.

When we returned to Nashville from our family visits, we pulled ourselves together and got ready to head to Italy, to give it our best shot.

Of course, like all good heist flicks, the plan was not without the occasional stumbling block.

AUGUST 14 — NO, MAKE THAT AUGUST 15

Usually we pack very light when we travel. This time, we took as many things over as we could, to get some personal items into our new place. I brought my guitar, which was quite a gamble for me. I wanted that guitar if we moved to Italy, of course, but if we didn't get the work visa, I sure would miss it in Nashville.

Ferragosto, August 15, is one of Italy's biggest holidays, and nearly every store is closed. We had planned to arrive in Italy the day before, the 14th, so we could do our shopping for the week. But weather delays forced us to stay overnight in Nashville in a dumpy airport hotel.

"Um, are you *sure?*" our cabbie asked us apprehensively, when we rolled up to the place. But we were more preoccupied with the tasks that laid ahead, so we tipped him and checked in. While Zen made about 30 calls to supermarkets in Italy before she identified one that would be open the next day (all while not touching the bedspread, or the carpet, or the floor), I dashed across the highway to a gas station to pick up some sandwiches and a six-pack of Dos Equis and a bottle of red wine. Zen eyed my over-purchase of booze with a mixture of disbelief and thankfulness. I sat and played guitar on the bed while we hoped not to get murdered in our shitty motor lodge.

The next day's flights worked as planned, and we arrived in Rome early on *Ferragosto*. We headed to the one open supermarket to get food, TP and other necessities — and ended up also buying a television. (Yes, we bought a TV at a grocery store.)

Arriving at our little apartment in Soriano, we found it stuffed with 21 boxes from IKEA. This was stuff we had ordered: a bed, patio chairs, and a chaise lounge for the "living room." But we also found that the previous owner's stuff was STILL THERE, mostly jammed into the upstairs space. Job One became figuring out how to get someone to remove all of the old, large furniture items that we wouldn't be needing. Zen suggested throwing it all over the balcony, but that might have been the jet lag talking. And everything was covered in a thin layer of dust and filth, remnants of the work the *muratore* crew had done.

Our first course of action was to clean the kitchen and bathroom, which were in pretty rough condition. (Due to our missed flight, we had been wearing the same clothes for 48 hours, so we were pretty rough too.) We spent a little time putting together some patio chairs for the terrace, so we'd have a place to sit and rest occasionally between all the cleaning and assembling and rearranging. Then we hoped to have enough energy to put together the bed, which was somewhere among those 21 boxes.

A few weeks before, when we'd purchased the furniture, it all seemed so romantic. We imagined we would solve the puzzle of the bed assembly together, maybe bond over it while drinking some wine. Then we'd dress it in the nicest crisp clean linens and enjoy a well-earned rest.

Real life: We were both exhausted at this point, and the bed had approximately eleventy-jillion parts. And since we had been in the same clothes for well over 48 hours, we were each trying to pretend that the other one didn't smell like hot melted gorgonzola on top of a rotting tuna carcass on the beach. The apartment had no air conditioning, so we kept all the windows open — which also invited mosquitoes to swarm us while we worked.

It was pretty late in the evening when we finally got the bed put together. We felt guilty about the construction noise as a way of introducing ourselves to our new neighbors, but we were desperate to have a place to sleep, so we hoped they didn't notice.

AUGUST 16

We woke in the morning to the sound of the town's 8am siren, followed by bells from the cathedral across the valley. In addition to furniture, the previous owner had left us a tremendous amount of random things. Some of it was really helpful — for example, four bottles of prosecco and a bottle of Aperol. Some of it was less than useful, such as a filthy toilet brush, a hair dryer you wear like a hat, and multiple jars of expired food. And all of it was dusty.

This day saw a major domestic breakthrough. The place had only a small dorm-sized fridge, and no range or washing machine. So we arranged for a stove, fridge, and washer to be delivered and hooked up. If you could see (and smell) what we looked (and smelled) like at this point, you would understand that the most important appliance was the washing machine.

I handled these transactions (in Italian) at a local shop. We thought about buying the appliances online and having them delivered, just to avoid having to stumble around in Italian, but ultimately we decided it was best to buy them in town. Everyone I spoke to was very patient and kind, despite the fact that we didn't always understand details about an appliance's safety/economy/features. Everything was delivered and installed that same afternoon, and I even got them to haul the old fridge away. These were significant expenses, among many that had us occasionally fretting about the overall cost of this endeavor. We alternated between reminding each other that this spending was an expected part of the "price of admission," and just submerging the topic in the previous owner's *prosecco*.

All of this cleaning and other work was exhausting in the heat, as we battled flies and mosquitoes. When Zen gets extremely tired, she sometimes also gets emotional about little things. That afternoon, she absolutely lost it when she couldn't get the plastic off of a hook she was trying to attach to the wall. That stupid sticky plastic was "trying to give her a stroke," she said, and she started crying over it.

While she was doing this, I had just been unpacking a suitcase, and I came across our pewter goblet. We are not religious, so when we got married in our backyard, we designed our own ceremony. Fourteen years earlier, we drank wine out of this goblet to complete our wedding ceremony.

To ease her stress, I put a little wine in the goblet and took her by the hand. We weaved our way through the maze of boxes and junk to the terrace, and we had a little drink together while looking at the sunset, as I held her in my arms. To mitigate the sappiness of the moment, I reminded her that at our wedding, a bug had landed in our wine cup, which I fished out with my finger before I drank it. Her tears turned to laughter and we ended the day on a high note.

AUGUST 17

At last, Marco had arranged for his cousin to load up and haul away a ton of stuff from our apartment. Three beds, including mattresses, a door and disassembled door frame, a giant window, a large porcelain pedestal sink, a large lamp, a huge plastic we-don't-even-know-what-the-hell kind of box, and a couple of large paintings and posters, as well as several boxes full of smaller items. (Did I mention that this apartment is only around 500 square feet?!) This was an insane amount of stuff to have in there, even before we had added our own bed and several other pieces of furniture.

Marco's cousin was none too happy with the amount of stuff, but he planned to either use it all himself, or give it to people who could use it. He expertly stuffed, tied, and wedged everything on top of his work truck. As he drove off, it looked like the Beverly Hillbillies were moving out. We breathed a huge sigh of relief — but not too deeply, because of all the dust that remained in the house. I do have a touch of asthma, after all.

Being professional cheapskates, we had found ways to refresh and reuse much of what remained. Everything that was unusable, we stuffed in our rental car — jam-packed with clothing, old magazines, makeup and hairspray, long-expired food from the previous owner, and a lot of the packaging material that came from the furniture we bought. (We had to drive all of this stuff around for several days before we were able to gain legal access to the dump.) Having so much stuff cleared out meant we could finally sweep and mop, and get some of the dirt and dust out of the place.

Then we resumed assembling our furniture. I usually love putting together IKEA furniture — I enjoy the puzzle aspect of it. I also like to take my time to do things properly and thoroughly, and then stand back and admire a job well done. But this night, as we were approaching sundown, I ended up in a pitched battle with an IKEA shelf. It shouldn't have been that difficult, but my state of mind was fragile, and I was arguing with the shelf as if it were sentient — and recalcitrant. "Quit f***ing doing that, asshole shelf!"

"You have to do it like my family always used to do jigsaw puzzles," Zen offered helpfully. "If the piece doesn't fit, use a box cutter to cut it to the right shape. It's an old family trick."

Then she pranced off happily to sweep the terrace and enjoy the view.

One of the funnier items we inherited from the previous owner was a bright yellow teddy bear candle. We spend every night by candlelight, preferring low light after years spent on concert stages, but this creepy bear was ... different. "Seeing his head on fire reminds me that I have a headache," Zen said when we first lit it up, "and the color reminds me that I have to pee." Nevertheless, when it started to get dark, it illuminated the house with a warm and beautiful light, making everything look cheery and homey. Until its face melted off and it collapsed on itself, that is.

Since the thing came with the house, we chose to chalk it up as an asset against the purchase price. This Italian custom of a house coming with many of the items of the previous owner (*"Tutto incluso!"*) took some getting used to, as it's not generally done in the US. But we were grateful for many of the things: They saved us a lot of money in furniture and housewares that we didn't have to purchase, which helped take the edge off of financial stress, and it made us feel more connected to the house, as if we had always been a part of its story.

AUGUST 18

This whole project worked in part because of Zen's ability to plan for months in advance, working out every detail with lists and diagrams and charts. "You're like the heist ringleader," I observed at one point.

"Yeah," she quipped, "but instead of some cool Clooney type, the ringleader wears yoga pants, uses curse words that would shame a sailor, and gets the plans stained with Cheeto dust."

But she made it all happen. One of the things she had anticipated was that without Wi-Fi or TV service, we'd want a way to watch movies to relax. So she packed our little DVD player and my Lord of the Rings discs. It was a treat, after a long day of cleaning and schlepping and cursing and sweating, to relax with a glass of wine and watch one of my favorite movies.

This apartment had no air conditioning, which is pretty typical throughout Europe, as it's extremely costly to run. "I'm a terrible, horrible, no-good person in the heat," Zen said (and who was I to argue?). It's especially vexing when we're hot and filthy and we have to do a lot of heavy lifting — when we're moving into an apartment, for example. But we were happy to discover that the summer in Soriano, especially after *Ferragosto,* is quite comfortable. It's warm in the day, maybe getting up to 90°F, but it cools off nicely in the evenings. And the humidity level is a tolerable level for human beings — unlike in Nashville, where it's like standing in front of a humidifier that is filled with human sweat all day long.

AUGUST 19

In the morning Zen got up early and made a very un-Italian breakfast, but one dear (and potentially damaging) to my heart: an assortment of cheesy eggs, sausage, and garlicky, peppery home fries. This was something she had made often when we were dating. "This breakfast is like 95 percent of why you married me in the first place, isn't it?" (I cannot confirm that percentage.)

After breakfast, we headed to the Questura, the police headquarters, which also handles immigration. Our lawyer had arranged an appointment for us to pick up a key element of our application for the work visa: that elusive *nulla osta*. We had a very narrow window in which to get this and everything else sorted; our lawyer had made it clear that this was our best and perhaps only chance to get this type of visa. Though the attorney had put the wheels in motion months earlier, the *nulla osta* had stalled over the summer. The guy who generates those at the Questura had not been at work for a month. But now "the guy" had returned, and the documents were ready.

Entering the Questura complex, we were baffled as to where to go. Every building was kind of gray and squat, and none of the doors were very clearly marked. We went through door after door, explaining in Italian what we were looking for. Each official we encountered gave us a different set of directions. At one point we ended up behind a gated police barrier (which was surely off-limits to civilians), and a few moments later we got hopelessly lost in a medical clinic.

Finally we found the immigration office. We entered a waiting room tightly packed with dozens of people in no discernable line. A digital board on the wall read "47." Zen took a number from the ticket dispenser — and pulled out "98." *D'oh!*

The office doors were propped open, letting the hot, humid air roll in. The in-wall air conditioner was hopelessly outgunned in this office full of hot, sweaty, annoyed people. A gaggle of workers, trying not to make eye contact with any of us, sorted papers behind what looked like bulletproof glass. Tons of grimy handprints and faceprints covered the glass, left by applicants like ourselves leaning against it in an effort to understand instructions from the officials.

We put our best smiles on and tried to look like we were having a great time — like we were *not* annoyed or sweaty or stressed AT ALL. Luckily, we have a ton of experience doing this, having sat under a variety of conductors of various skill levels over our careers.

The number on the digital reader never changed.

But our strategy of looking unbothered and eager actually worked! We got called up after I "accidentally" made eye contact with a worker. (Who? Me? *Us?* Oh, could we come up there? Oh, okay, we'd love to — *sure!)* At the same time we saw a different applicant in the corner with another officer, literally yelling at them for being stupid. We preferred our strategy.

We got up to the window, behind which the clerk had spread out our documents, including the prized *nulla osta*. Right away, Zen noticed, reading upside-down, that they had spelled her name wrong — ZANeba instead of ZENeba. She turned her head my direction and anxiously whispered, "My name is wrong."

My breakfast threatened to make a reappearance. I had that feeling you get when falling off a cliff in a dream — that the center of your body is suddenly empty, that sickening feeling of fast, unstoppable descent. Zen floated the idea that maybe it would be easier if she just legally changed her name to match the new document. The two of us began one of our whose-flop-sweat-stinks-more competitions. I tried talking as slowly as I could to the official to buy time. We did not want to step away from the desk and lose our place in line, because the office might close before we got called again. Zen frantically dialed our lawyer as I flailed and tried to be charming.

After the second attempt, our lawyer answered, despite the fact that he was on the beach in his Speedo. I handed over the phone to the official, apologizing again for the wait. After a few moments, they determined that we need to get the *Camera di Commercio* (Chamber of Commerce) to fix the typo, then return to the Questura with the corrected document.

"Va bene, ora andiamo lì?" I asked — Okay, we go there now?

Purtroppo no. Unfortunately not — the *Camera di Commercio* is only open on Wednesday.

All right, so we go there tomorrow, then come back here?

Again: *No.* The immigration office isn't open tomorrow; you need to come back here on Thursday once the form is fixed tomorrow.

So back to Soriano we drove, where we spent the next 18 hours uselessly chatting about whether or not the other office would be able to fix it. Will they *really* be open? Will the Questura accept a corrected document? Did the chicken really come before the egg? Who put that chocolate in my peanut butter? Each rhetorical question sparked long discussions amounting to nothing other than keeping us both from having a panic attack.

We tried to distract ourselves with the continuing task of setting things up in the apartment. There was plenty to do, at least.

Years ago we stopped giving each other holiday and birthday gifts, opting instead to choose crafts by local artists we discovered on our travels. To make this place feel more homey, we had shipped ourselves a big box of such things: a blown glass plate from Venice, a ceramic hand-painted ceramic tile that says *"bagno"* for our bathroom door, a pair of pottery coffee mugs from Ireland, and an English stained glass window in a wooden frame. Zen had the idea to mount this with some metal chains onto a wood beam the *muratore* had installed — the glass became a stand-in for a wall between the bed and the living room space. At dawn on clear days, the sun beams through the stained glass to awaken us.

While I worked on hanging the window, Zen tried to spruce up a few of the old items that had been left to us. She spent a good bit of time on the terrace painting the metal frame of an old table. "It's so nice to paint when cats aren't around," she remarked. "Nobody's sticking their tail in the paint tray!" (Yes, that has happened to us before. Thanks, Mr. Weasely!)

It was a funny comment, but it was also a reminder: In the event we were successful in getting our work visas, we would have just under another week to get the place fit to live in. If we were lucky, the next time we walked into this house in November, we would be living here. Everything needed to be ready — not just adequate for the two of us, but also meeting the exacting living standards of our four fussy feline overlords.

AUGUST 20

We had some time before we needed to head to the *Camera di Commercio* to fix our documents, so in the morning we did a sweep and a mop — each day this became easier as we unpacked and assembled and sorted and discarded more items in the house. We mounted a few more tiles on the wall: some of our prized ceramic pieces from Tuscany that had been mounted in our kitchen in Nashville, that we had removed to bring them back to their "home" in Italy. We also hung our framed CDs, the discs we produced with ALIAS Chamber Ensemble — Zen was the artistic director for 16 years, and these CDs were the hard-won products of our labors. Bit by bit, it was beginning to feel like we belonged here.

But did we belong here, really? That remained to be determined. We drove back to Viterbo to the Chamber of Commerce, a beautiful stone building in the town center. Inside, the atmosphere was officious but clearly historic, with that old-books smell you find in the most magnificent libraries.

We first encountered Italian Wilford Brimley, the security guard, who heard our story and directed us to an office down a hall. There, several men heatedly discussed the issue; Zaneba — I mean, Zeneba — calmly and meekly assured them that she was pretty sure her name had two Es in it. "Meek" is not usually her thing exactly, so I admired her Oscar-worthy performance, especially knowing how stressed she was. I knew that in her mind she was screaming, "Goddammit, I KNOW how to spell my NAME!"

After about 10 minutes, it was determined that another official needed to correct the mistake, so Wilford Brimley led us down another corridor. He waited patiently with us in the hallway for about 20 minutes while the relevant official finished up her previous meeting. We passed the time by chatting with the guy about the town he lives in, the festivals there, great food in the area, music, politics, history... all things we can discuss in Italian with relative ease. It was a great relief to have a conversation in Italian that we could manage, rather than the ones we had been struggling with for the past week: gas lines, legal documents, electric service bills, roofing tiles — those conversations really took us to the end of our language ability.

When we sat down with the official, our strategy of patience, gratitude, and lighthearted banter paid off, and several bumps were ironed out. Though multiple times she seemed to hit a roadblock, our method of looking at her like a dog begging for bacon seemed to motivate her to take care of us.

Ultimately we walked out of there with our paperwork corrected and stamped. We considered it a qualified success — we still had to return to the Questura the next day, but for now, we thanked everyone profusely and returned yet again to Soriano to resume our furniture assembly, and our unpacking and cleaning.

Later that afternoon, we were startled by a piercing BUZZZZ! It was the doorbell, and it scared the bejeezus out of us. This was the first time we had heard it — we hadn't been aware until that moment that we had one. Was this a delivery? Were we expecting other packages? We didn't even know anymore.

But it was our next-door neighbor Giuseppina, dropping off a huge string of tomatoes from her garden. She knew we had been scrambling with our home project, and she wanted to make sure we at least had something to eat. These acts of generosity and kindness from our neighbors truly overwhelmed us, again and again.

AUGUST 21

We showed up bright and early to the immigration office. We were the first ones in line, they immediately stamped our papers and... then I woke up out of a fitful sleep, because nothing ever works like that, does it?

We woke to another random food delivery from one of our neighbors. Pietro, Giuseppina's *babbo* (dad) came to our door with a giant bucket full of ripe figs that he had just picked at his country farm. He asked if we would like some. We tried to take three, but he insisted that we take nine. (He was pretty disappointed that we settled for only nine.)

We asked him if there's a recipe that he prefers for these. He just shrugged and took a fig out of his bucket and popped it in his mouth. *"Màgnali!"* he said, which in the Sorianese dialect means "Eat them!" We didn't know that at the time, but the general meaning was obvious.

One of Zen's projects that morning was attaching a magnet under a shelf to hold her chef's knife. She superglued a few magnets together, then glued them to the underside of the cabinet. It took her a while to figure out how many magnets would be required to keep the knives secured. Meanwhile, the knife kept falling from its suspended position onto the counter. Her tendency to superglue her fingers alternately to the glue container and to each other added to the difficulty. Much cursing ensued, continuing the lesson in American profanities that our neighbors had been receiving this past week or so.

When Zen finally managed to get the magnet (and, more importantly, the knife) to stay put, she tried to take a picture to document the process. She had been posting a lot of the little details of our "housewarming" on our social media as it progressed. But she had to get me to open her phone, since it no longer recognized her fingerprint through the glue.

After our coffee, we headed back to Viterbo for the third time. We'd memorized the route by then, and the trip was a breeze.

We walked into the Questura office — more crowded than it was the last time, and hotter, too. Despite having had an appointment for this return trip, we waited for an hour or more — always with our best non-stressed smiles plastered to our faces, even though our clothes gradually became plastered to our bodies from the heat. Finally an official behind the window recognized us, and beckoned for us to approach the window and hand over our paperwork.

She scanned it all, then called one of her colleagues over. A quiet but rapid-fire discussion ensued. Then they called over *yet another* colleague to join in the talks. The three of them held their summit for what seemed like an eternity — in reality it was 15 minutes — before breaking up. Our official came back to the window with our papers. *"A posto."*

We got wide-eyed. *"A posto?"*

She smiled back at our dumb, eager faces. *"A posto!"* The documents were all in order!

She filed their copies and handed us our *nulla osta* papers, signed and sealed. A wave of relief washed over us — we still had a chance at the work visa! We determined not to let these papers out of our sight until we got to the Consulate in Detroit the following month.

As we walked out, Zen muttered under her breath, "You can have my *nulla osta* when you pry it from my cold, dead hands."

AUGUST 22

The next few days were a flurry of activity, as we scrambled to tie up loose ends with the apartment. The next part of our "heist movie" was to get a heater installed. If our application for a work visa went as we hoped, we'd be coming back in November, at which point it would be quite cold.

We had ordered a wood-burning *stufa* (stove heater) from a big-box online company — fire-engine red, with a little bread oven on top. It was another of these romantic ideas: We'd heat our house with wood, maybe even with logs we gathered ourselves in the beechwood forest on the mountain! And we'd bake our own Italian bread in the oven compartment — energy-efficient *and* adorable!

The company had given us a four-day window in which they might deliver it, and no other tracking information, so we had to be home for a solid 96 hours. I made a mental note never again to complain about Comcast customer service. While we awaited the *stufa* delivery, we continued organizing the place. Storage space was at a minimum — there was no closet, for example — so we had to be mindful of how things were set up. There was not an inch — or, rather, a centimeter — to spare!

When we had first seen our tiny apartment, it had a few interior walls, which made it really boxy, dark, and stuffy. One of the things we had asked the *muratore* to do, in between April and August, was to knock down two of the walls, leaving one as a sort of partition between bed and foyer.

In May, Gabriele texted us a picture of the work in progress. Looking at it, we couldn't even tell what we were seeing until we realized... he had taken down *all* the walls! We had obviously failed to communicate — and we had no doubt the fault was ours.

That's how we ended up with the "open plan" layout we were now working with. When we first decided to undertake the project of this apartment, the two of us agreed that we'd have to let go of a lot of control, and to extend a ton of trust. This project would have been impossible if we insisted on asserting a single "perfect" vision that could not be deviated from, and this wall was a perfect example of that.

Years earlier, we had coined a word to refer to this kind of experience:

"fuck·er·tu·ni·ty" / 'fuh-kr 'TOO-neh-tee/ *(noun)* [2015 - first known use]
> - **an event that at first seems terrible or disadvantageous, but makes things ultimately turn out better than they otherwise would have.**

The unexpected wall removal turned out to be a benefit — we set up backless shelves that created a barrier without blocking light, which added some vital storage space. This turned out to be the first of many "fuckertunities" in this incredible adventure.

After we assembled the last of the shelves and stacked them up to build the "wall," Zen sent me out to buy some prosciutto and mozzarella from the local *alimentari* (food shop). When I returned, she put together a little lunch on the terrace, using a cantaloupe, some tomatoes, and some local olive oil that a neighbor had dropped off the day before: *Prosciutto e melone* and an *insalata caprese* — perfect snacks for a warm summer day. We sat on the terrace, enjoying the break from the dust and clutter, and tried to imagine what actual life would be like here. It was starting to feel like home.

AUGUST 25

We received notice from the *corrieri* that, after a series of snafus that had delayed the shipment, they would be delivering our *stufa* the following day, which was welcome news. Not only would we get our pellet stove, but knowing that it wasn't coming that day released us from the Great Stufa Vigil of 2019 and allowed us to leave the house. We had gotten a ton of work done over the past two days, but the constant cleaning, dusting, mopping, and unpacking, had all taken their toll, especially since we were doing it while being bombarded by mosquitoes. We also had a list of stuff we needed from the DIY home store: cleaners, nuts and bolts, sponges... and the big ticket item, a gas grill for the terrace.

We were sticking within our budget for new-house purchases, and yet the seemingly endless money-hemorrhaging made us wince and grit our teeth on a daily basis. But when we got in the car, Zen said: "I don't care if mosquito screens are a million dollars. We are buying them for every fucking window." Poor Zen was the primary magnet for the *zanzare* (mosquitoes), which skipped over me to cluster around her. The bites affected her differently from the way they did in the US, where they were a temporary annoyance. Here, each bite swelled into an itchy, hard, red welt that she would scratch open in her sleep. After a few days, she was covered in crusty, itchy scabs. It was all very romantic, we joked to each other, as we both worried about her ability to get past US Border Patrol covered in open festering wounds.

At the DIY store, we bought a dual gas grill, which could be converted to use *metano* from the city line instead of *propano* from a tank. We did our best to follow the Italian instructions to change out the hardware, hoping not to blow ourselves up while grilling our first steak. When we finished, there were several extra screws and random parts remaining that had not been mentioned in the instructions, which did not inspire confidence, but our *idraulico* (plumber) stopped by to check the work. *"Sembra a posto, bravo,"* he said after examining the gas fittings — It seems in place. Success! We could now cook outside without fear of explosions.

While we were doing all of this work on the place, the details of our lives were proceeding as ever in the US. Every day we took care of a dozen e-mails — booking recording sessions, organizing our schedules with the symphony calendar and ensemble rehearsals, and assorted other business. Despite what seemed like a dreamy (albeit dusty) experience in Italy, we never lost sight of the fact that we still had jobs, obligations, cats! And we knew that pulling off this Big Idea was still a long-shot.

Next, I set out to get some major "husband points" and installed all the mosquito screens. As I put up the last of the screens, we heard a voice at the door. *"Matteo, Matteo..."* It was our neighbor, stopping by with more garden bounty — this time, a humongous bucket of grape tomatoes.

We already had received a lot of tomatoes as gifts from other neighbors — everyone had huge surpluses at this time of year. So Zen decided to make a tomato sauce while I took a short walk to a local butcher to buy some of their house-made sausages. When I returned, the whole house was filled with delicious sauce aroma: garlic, onions, and fresh tomatoes, mixed together with a touch of red wine.

While the sauce percolated, I sat out on the balcony with my guitar, picking and singing a bit, as I kept an eye on the pork sausages on the grill. The sun was beginning to set, the sky turning a cotton candy color. I took a moment to appreciate the mountain peaks in the distance, far away, across Umbria, in Abruzzo. I heard Sante's goats bleating below, in their pasture surrounded by olive groves.

"It sounds like they're saying "Maaa-aaatt!" Zen called from inside. "Do they like the music, or are they asking you to stop?" she teased me.

AUGUST 26

The good news was, we finally knew when the *stufa* was coming. The bad news was, that day, we had to drive to Tuscany that day for a meeting with our immigration lawyer, to get the paperwork together to present to the Consulate in Detroit in

September. This appointment was all part of the needle-threading process we had to do to apply for our work visas, and we could not reschedule it by an hour, let alone by a day or two. We had planned this trip as an overnight, in part to give ourselves a few hours break, and in part because we knew we wouldn't be safe to do all that driving in one day.

We hired a friend — Dane, the brother of the aforementioned Hamish — to wait in our apartment for the delivery. He too is totally bilingual, having lived in Soriano since childhood, so he could handle things much more easily than we could. He'd be there to take delivery and then coordinate with Simone, our *idraulico*, who would install the *stufa*.

We were driving up the Autostrada when Dane called. "Hi guys. They delivered the *stufa*..."

"Great!" we said.

"Ah, not really, it's a pretty big mess," he replied. Through the days of delayed delivery, it had been unsalvageably damaged. All the metal parts were dented, Dane told us. The glass window was broken, and some of the heating stones inside were in pieces.

The *corrieri* had already left. There was nothing else we could do at this point, so we thanked our friend and proceeded with our trip. That evening at the hotel we'd send messages to the company (to ask for a refund) and to the *corrieri* (to arrange for them to come and pick it up), but first we continued to Firenze. We resolved to go to the local *stufa* shop when we returned to Soriano and buy whatever model they could install by November, regardless of cost. Lesson learned: Always buy local.

We parked outside Firenze's town walls and walked into the office of our *avvocato*. Our lawyer again reviewed the process for us, assuring us that we'd be successful if we did everything exactly as he said and exactly according to the schedule.

Back out on the street in Firenze, the moment felt surreal. The next step was the consulate in Detroit. And then everything would either fizzle out, or move very, very quickly.

Paperwork in hand, we got back to our car and drove up into the Casentino mountains in northeast Tuscany, where we would be staying at a little *albergo* in a small mountain town. We were there in particular to go to one of our favorite restaurants, a delicious diversion between our lawyer's office and Soriano. We had only one more full day before returning to the US, and we had to resolve StufaGate. But for now, we ordered a nice bottle of Chianti, indulged in some paper-thin *pappardelle* with wild boar sauce, and topped it off with a creamy *panna cotta* drizzled with caramel, then rolled ourselves off to bed.

We awoke to the sound of birds and the smell of pine, reminding us we were in the mountains of the Casentino. A quick espresso, one last deep breath of mountain air, and then back to the grind, to finish our heist.

AUGUST 27

Upon returning to Soriano the next day, we discovered our driveway littered with little pieces of the *stufa* — a piece of glass here, a chunk of metal there.

We called, e-mailed, texted, Messenger-ed and WhatsApp-ed the delivery company to arrange them to pick up this now-very-expensive piece of garbage. This seemed like an incredibly complex operation to sort out, but eventually they arrived at the top of our street in a large delivery truck. I walked up to where they were parked. The driver explained the problem to me — shouted at me, really, in rapid Italian, the only part of which I understood clearly were the more colorful and less-than-friendly words he used.

The upshot, roughly translated: They couldn't f***ing drive down our c***ing street, the truck was too g****mn big, and they'd only take it if we'd f***ing schlep the thing up to the top of the street.

I'm a quick learner. Copying his colorful verbiage, I agreed to f***ing schlep it up there, but it would take us a c***ing while. He said Okay, they'd maybe f***ing come back in the afternoon if they could, to pick it up. And then they f***ing drove off.

With great difficulty, and vastly exceeding our actual strength, Zen and I managed to hoist this bulky 250-pound piece of junk into our rental car — luckily, we happened to have a hatchback. We managed to do this without scratching the rental, but it did cost some blood and bruises on our part, and our neighbors learned a raft of new and filthy colorful verbiage in English. Because of all the one-way streets, we had to drive it all the way around and through town to come through to the right part of the street where the delivery guys could pick it up when they returned. We eased it out of the car and left it standing on the side of the street above our house.

We had asked Simone, our *idraulico,* to help us communicate with the *corrieri.* They kept changing their return time. We were extremely concerned: We didn't know if we could be charged by the city for dumping garbage on a public street, but we were afraid to find out the hard way. This was not the way we envisioned introducing ourselves to the neighborhood. As the day approached sundown, though, we looked out the window — and the *stufa* was gone!

Simone called us a few minutes later and told us the *corrieri* would be there shortly. *"Ummm… Già loro hanno venuti,"* I said — They had already come and taken the *stufa.* He seemed confused, and told us to hang on; then he called back a few minutes later.

"Ciao, Matteo… Ascolta: La stufa era rubato." Listen, Matt: It was stolen.

We sat silently for a moment — but then Zen started wildly clapping and gleefully exclaimed: "Great — it's gone!" We sent a note to the company: We left it for pickup for the *corrieri,* and it's now no longer our problem. No matter the arguing we might have to do with the company (or with our credit card), it was a great relief that we could scratch this off of our To Do list.

I was bitter about the day's events and stressed about the possibility that we'd have to pay for the *stufa* anyway. Zen came over, rubbed my shoulders, and said "Don't worry, sweetheart," and poured me a big plastic cup full of red wine.

Ah, Italy.

AUGUST 28

This was our last full day in Italy on this trip. The "happy ending" of our appliance being destroyed and then stolen was darkened by the fact that we still needed to find a way to heat our house — in one day.

After visiting a couple of big-box stores in nearby Viterbo (of which we were wary, but at least we were on the ground instead of online), we became demoralized. Nothing even close to what we had been looking for existed in our price range and — at least as importantly — our size range.

In our local travels over the past week or so, we had noticed that there was indeed a local shop a five-minute drive away, out in the country between towns. It was late afternoon — in fact we had just heard Soriano's siren very faintly in the distance — so it was really now or never. "Let's check it out," Zen said. "What do we have to lose?"

The shop was a family-run place — an actual mom and pop greeted us when we entered their showroom. There were all manner of chimneys and fireplaces and *stufe* and barbecues and outdoor pizza ovens — it made us wish we had a few hundred square meters (and a couple hundred thousand bucks) to play with. As it was, we homed in on the smallest *stufa* they had, which was a pellet stove. Wood pellets are a common method of heating in Italy, and while it wasn't the romantic wood-burner we had been thinking about, it seemed cute and extremely easy to operate and maintain, and to afford. (A bonus point: Due to one of our dear Mr. Weasely's various medical conditions, we'd already been using pine pellets as cat litter for years. "As long as we don't mix up the stuff we're going to burn with the stuff that was already peed on," Zen quipped.)

We discussed our needs and our situation with the proprietors, including the possibility that we might be moving there in the winter, so we needed to organize something to get set up in the next couple of months.

How long will you be living in this place? the woman asked us.

"Speriamo per sempre," Zen answered. *"Fino moriamo."* — Forever, we hope, until we die. The *signora* chuckled at this, but her husband shook his head and crossed himself with great seriousness.

We needed to talk about delivery and installation. The fact that we were already working with an *idraulico* was a big advantage — they could coordinate a delivery with him and he could install it any time in the near future. But they wanted to discuss it with him directly, so we gave Simone a call and handed our phone over to the couple.

They discussed in what seemed like great detail, until the *signora* handed my phone back. *"Lui viene,"* she said. He was coming to the shop! They also called their daughter, who spoke some English and lived nearby, to come in and translate. She arrived just a few minutes later.

Simone had been giving his twin 4-year-old girls a bath before putting them to bed, after which he'd come by to discuss *stufa* details. When he arrived, we did our best to follow their conversation, into which we only occasionally interjected ourselves. The coordination of delivery and installation was sorted out quickly and easily. The main question was whether or not the *stufa* we had picked out was going to be big enough. This involved extensive discussion from everyone: mother, father, daughter, Simone, and peripherally, us, discussing what we should end up with.

Simone assumed that since we were Americans, we'd want

to crank the heat to an extreme degree. And the husband thought we'd need something bigger, with more bells and whistles, perhaps not grasping how small our place was (or, again, our cheapskate factor). We said we didn't need it that warm, but no one seemed to believe us.

But soon the *signora* intervened and interrupted the two men. "They said their place is small, they don't need it to be a very high temperature. Let them get the small one that they like!" There was no feeling of being "upsold." It was clear that everyone was worried that we would freeze in our home if we didn't get a big enough *stufa*. We knew from experience that most Italians seem to like their homes heated to the point where you could grow a palm tree in the bedroom, so we understood why they were concerned. But it was clear we were not getting anywhere in the discussion.

Finally I saw Zen get that gleam in her eye she gets when she has figured something out, and she said "Unfortunately, we can't have it too hot in the house. It is bad for the violin and cello." SOLD! The instruments became our scapegoats and the discussion was ended. As we started to sign the documents, Zen pointed to the fancy *stufa* that the father had been showing us. *"Solo voglio quello se c'è anche un parte crematorio, se..."* — I only want that one if it has a crematorium feature... You know, if... She left the thought hang in the air. The poor guy's eyes nearly popped out of his head and he feverishly crossed himself again, while his wife winked at us and chuckled.

"A posto," she said. *"Facciamo tutto facilmente."* We paid for the *stufa* and discussed annual maintenance, which would be done by their son, just a personal phone call away — another benefit to buying local. Simone discussed contact and delivery information with the couple, everyone shook hands, and we left the shop. There in the parking lot, we talked with Simone about how much we'd pay him to do the installation, and gave him a copy of our key. We'd leave him the cash on the table inside the

door, and he could get the work done at his leisure. It was another instance of placing trust in people, and another instance where we were richly rewarded for doing so.

"Va bene, d'accordo," he said — Okay, agreed. As we parted, thanking Simone profusely, he added, *"Speriamo di vederci a novembre... buona fortuna!"* — We hope we'll see you in November! We did too.

On our way back to the apartment we stopped at a little gift shop in Soriano, where we bought two plush teddy bears. When we got back to the house, we put an envelope full of cash in a little basket by the door, along with these two bears — gifts for Simone's daughters, whose bedtime we had interrupted.

In retrospect, the switch from the "romantic" wood stove to the pellet type was better for us in the long run. As we've subsequently been told countless times by neighbors, gathering and storing wood is no small task, nor is running a wood stove for the purpose of heating. If we were to grow old in this place, the pellets would be much easier to manage. The broken and stolen *stufa* turned out to be yet another fuckertunity.

And thus our "heist" was pulled off. All our documents were in order, the apartment equipped and cleaned and organized, heating apparatus bought and installation arranged. We headed back to the US... Roll the credits!

Now we just had to jump through a thousand more hoops to see if we'd ever get to actually live there.

CHAPTER 6
Limbo: Waiting For Detroit

SEPTEMBER 2019

*B*ACK IN THE US, it was a strange time for us. The symphony season started up as usual, and while our colleagues knew that we had bought a little place in Italy, they had no idea that wheels were turning that could lead to us soon quitting our jobs and moving out of the country, and very soon. To all outside appearances, there was nothing different about us, but inside we were roiling with excitement and trepidation and uncertainty.

Meanwhile, we managed to arrange for the time off we needed to make our September 17 appointment in Detroit. We also bought another ticket to return to Italy. One of the requirements for a work visa was that the applicant have a paid-for plane ticket to be in Italy within 90 days of the visa being granted. So we had to buy tickets, in the hopes that we'd be successful. If we failed, it would cost us a few hundred bucks more to alter it for some future trip.

We also needed to coordinate our (potential) trip overseas with a pet shipper. We had identified an outfit that could handle all of the relevant paperwork for moving animals overseas: customs documents, carrier parameters, medical records. The flight itself had to be one that was suited to carry animals in the cargo hold, because only one of our cats could travel in the passenger cabin with us.

The shipper reviewed the flights we were considering, and indicated which ones were on planes that could accommodate animals. This is not a standard filter you can apply when searching flights on Orbitz. Moreover, the date could not be too far into the cold months — airlines won't allow pets in their holds if temperatures are consistently below a certain level. In the end, we bought tickets for November 18, which was within our extremely narrow window of opportunity. It was a lot of trouble — and expense — to organize the transport of these animals. But we don't have kids — our cats are our babies, and we are slaves to their well-being.

Our Realtor — the guy who had sold us our house in Nashville back in 2005 — was one of the few people we told about our plan. We asked him if we could have the house ready to sell in the event that we were approved. This was no problem, he said, but we'd have to clean the place up and get professional pictures taken. We made it clear that it would have to be sold with all of our stuff still in the house: no staging, no empty rooms, no aerosol spray smelling like cookies. Just our million dusty books, our cat-scratched furniture, and in fact our cats still in the house, blocked off in one little bedroom upstairs. This is not the ideal way to run an open house, we understood, but it was the only way we could manage the situation.

He sent his photographer to take photos — *ka-ching!* another possibly pointless expense — and arranged for several different kinds of inspections — *ka-ching, ka-ching, ka-ching!* We hired a landscaper to dress up our back yard — something we normally did ourselves, but we were too busy with work. So... *ka-ching!* The spending was stressing us out. Plane tickets that we might not use; pictures of a house we might not sell; cat carriers we might never put on a plane. On top of what to us was a huge output of funds for the apartment in Italy, the daily trickle involved in this project was hard for a couple of cheapskates to weather.

Over the years, we had started an annual tradition of getting rid of stuff in our house. Before we started dating, Zeneba and I both lived in small apartments with minimal possessions, so we could pack up and move quickly. In fact, my apartment was so spartan that the building manager would sometimes use it as a model unit to show prospective new renters when I wasn't in town, since it was basically empty.

Once we bought our house together, we somehow seemed to accumulate things to fill up the space. We always recognized that it was a position of privilege, to have so many possessions that it becomes overwhelming, but it began to feel weighty — the storage of things, the clutter, the dust. So we started an Annual Purge, selling or giving away unused things. We also instituted a "buy something, lose something" policy: If we did purchase anything new, we'd have to get rid of something else equal in size or clutter. We recognized the immense privilege that we could get rid of a lot of things and not even miss them.

Our travels encouraged this mindset. When we'd go overseas, we traveled light, and we realized these were some of the best times of our lives, even though we lacked all the "stuff" that seemed so necessary at home. We began to look at things differently, and wonder why we had so much stuff to begin with. Nevertheless, we still managed to accumulate lots of things, so we had a ton of work to do. We ramped up our effort to get rid of stuff — yard sale, online selling, and the occasional fobbing off something onto friends. ("Hey, bud... You know what would look great? You, in this Tyrolean hat!") Our book collection was a huge shelf of memories — and dust mites. We went through the process gradually, taking a couple of boxes every few weeks to sell at a local bookshop. At one point we had sold or donated 11 boxes of books, and that barely impacted the array on our shelves.

The days ticked by. We went to work — none of our colleagues knew of our plans — and we waited for the day to arrive for us to fly to Detroit and present our application. Every few days, we checked and re-checked — and re-re-checked — our documents, making sure we had everything in order. Included in the required paperwork was a USPS Priority mailer with prepaid stamps so they could return our documents (including our passports, which we were required to leave with them) at some point afterward. "Hey, guess what?" Zen piped up one day. "If they don't give us the visa, and they forget to mail our passports back, we can't use these nonrefundable tickets!" She proceeded to pour a big fat glass of wine.

We had the first appointment of the day at the Consulate in Detroit at 9 am on September 17, so we had arranged to fly from Nashville the day before, rent a car, and stay in the Financial District within easy walking distance to the building. We wanted to be within walking distance as a precaution, in case of traffic. The whole flight up, we went over our "pitch" again and again: What we were proposing; our background as concert organizers and performers and Grammy-nominated chamber music recording artists and producers; the many big-name musicians we had played with over the years; why we were suited to live in Italy and apply our knowledge and artistry to creating events in Italy and add to the cultural life there. Our *avvocato* had said we should do the meeting in English, but if we wanted, we could drop a few Italian phrases here and there to show that we knew a little something. It was just like a presentation for an arts grant, something we had done dozens of times. We were as prepared as we knew how to be.

We got our car and drove into town. Neither of us knew Detroit, and though it wasn't why we were there, we thought we'd do a little sightseeing. We tried to visit the lakeside, but it seemed that everything was privatized — homes or yacht clubs. We failed to find a stretch of lakefront that was open to the public, so we gave up and headed downtown to check into our Airbnb. It was the apartment home of an elderly lady — she had evacuated the place just for our stay. She had not, however, evacuated her collection of weird, creepy antique dolls, who stared at us from every shelf and corner of the place.

Not wanting to hang out with the dolls more than necessary, we headed out to dinner at a hip cocktail bar. (More for the cocktails than the dinner — we really needed to keep our jitters in check.) We asked the server about the lakefront. "Yeah, you have to know where to go," he explained, "or else have a lot of money." Neither point applied to us, unfortunately. But no worries. Some bar snacks and drinks had us feeling pretty good; and again, we were as prepared as we could be for this appointment in the morning.

We decided to check all of our papers once more before we went to bed. Everything was in order and accounted for. Wait. "Umm, where's..." I stammered.

"Where's what?" Zen asked, her voice rising in response to the stress she heard in mine.

I couldn't find the mailer stamps.

Without the stamps, the mailer was useless, and without that, the Consulate wouldn't take the application. We went through every pocket in every bag and item of clothing we had; opened every folder and flipped through every set of documents. They were nowhere to be found.

The owner's dolls seemed to be grinning at us now — mocking us. We started panicking. To think that our whole operation up to this point — all the list-making and calendar-scheduling and finely tuned clockwork and needle-threading and chainsaw-juggling — to think that all of that could come to nothing for want of a couple of eight-dollar stamps? It was more than we could bear. ("Don't say it, stupid dolls! Don't say a goddamn word." They didn't, but they *really* looked like they wanted to.)

With all the searching and flailing and paper-rifling, it was well past 1 am. We scrambled online to look up the nearest USPS with a self-service kiosk. It was about 15 blocks away, and it opened at 8:30 am. Too far to walk. We had planned things so that we could just get out of bed and clean up and walk to the appointment, leaving our car until afterward. But now we'd have to drive to the post office, then drive back to the Consulate and park the car for our 9 am meeting, all during rush hour in a town we didn't know at all. I mapped it out, checking different routes to and from the post office, hoping that traffic didn't add too much time.

It would have to do. Despite the stress, we managed to sleep a good 10 or 15 minutes.

We got up and showered and packed, then drove down to the post office, getting there five minutes (which seemed like five hours) before they opened the door. When we got in, we puzzled over the automated kiosk for what seemed like another hour (probably two minutes), finally managing to buy two Priority stamps. We got in the car, pulled an illegal U-turn ("I can't believe you did that, Boy Scout!" Zen teased, ever-hilarious even under pressure), and drove our carefully studied route to the garage next to the Consulate office building.

We arrived, to our surprise, a few minutes early. Not wanting to appear like stalkers outside their office door, we hung back in the lobby for a bit, to collect ourselves and do a little extra last-minute preparation. This was the Buhl Building, one of those neo-gothic office buildings from the 1920s, and the lobby was old-school: lots of wood and marble and glass, a lingering smell of a hundred years of stale tobacco and stale coffee. When it was time, we entered one of those old-timey elevators and ascended to the Consulate offices.

We presented our appointment papers, filled out a form, and stepped up to speak to an official through an unremarkable service window. She flipped through our file of papers and took our passports. If all went well, those would be sent back to us with the visa embossed on one of the pages. She paused a moment on our *nulla osta* — we could see the spot where Zen's name correction glared at us like a nasty pimple. But the official just nodded to herself and moved on. Zen and I exchanged a glance. She exhaled a deep breath of relief, and I tried like hell to keep my knees from wobbling as we stood there.

"And what is your work visa for?" the official asked.

Ah—the moment of truth. "We're professional classical musicians with decades of experience, and we'll be working with communities and institutions to create and organize cultural events and..."

"Okay, that's nice," she interrupted, still flipping through the paperwork. Then she looked at the return envelopes and the stamps. "That all looks fine, good."

The official jotted something on a sticky note, stuck it to our file, put everything in a larger envelope, tossed it into an "in-basket" on the desk behind her, and said, "Okay, you're all set. Look for the return in a few weeks."

"Uh..." I replied intelligently.

That was it. We thanked her and walked out the door. We were silent as we rode the elevator down, left the building and walked up to our car in the garage. After such a long run-up to this moment, it felt anticlimactic. No sit-down in a meeting room with overstuffed leather chairs, no sales pitch extolling our credentials and visions as musicians and concert organizers, no questions about whether we had a place to live or why we knew Italy or how we found our town or what was our favorite monastic *liquore*. Just a "Don't call us, we'll call you."

We sent a message to our *avvocato*, to tell him it was done. He called us back right away. "Congratulations!" he exclaimed. "Now we just wait." Was it a bad sign that they didn't ask any questions, didn't discuss our proposal at all, didn't even want to know if we could speak Italian or how much we love the Italian culture? "No, as long as they read the application, you should be fine. *Auguri,*" he added. *"Ciao!"*

We sat in the car for a few minutes, stunned. Zen cried a little, and I tried not to. Then we drove back to the airport, dropped the car off, checked in for our flight back to Nashville, and drank what under the circumstances seemed like a perfectly normal number of Blue Moon ales.

Back at work the next morning, we were zombies. It had been a surreal 24 hours — more so because we were severely sleep-deprived from the stamp snafu two nights earlier. Yet still we could tell no one. The days dragged on as we awaited a response. Meanwhile we continued our "stuff sell-off," our jobs, our daily business.

It seemed like many weeks, but it was only 10 days later when our daily morning check of the USPS tracking site indicated that our envelope had been sent from Detroit. Zen had the smart (and totally not-at-all stalker-like) idea to send the Consulate a message via Facebook: We see the envelope has been mailed with our passports. Can you tell us if the visa was approved?

An official from the Consulate responded surprisingly quickly: "I believe so; I'll check and let you know."

It was like someone from the lottery commission knocking on our door and saying "Hi, I'm happy to inform you that... hang on, I have to take this call."

Pins and needles. Hours went by. (Well, okay, 20 minutes.) We were watching the clock. We had to leave shortly for work. We were just accepting that we'd have to wait until our lunch break at least, when... *"Ding!"*

"Yes, the visas have been issued and sent out."

We reread the message again and again to make sure there was no ambiguity. Nope, it looks like we got it.

We got it!

We linked arms and jumped up and down in our living room like kids on a trampoline.

Then we hopped on our scooters and went to our jobs at the symphony hall. As I sat down onstage with my cello, I sent a quick e-mail to our Realtor: "List the house." All through the rehearsal we were sure our colleagues knew we were up to something, given the wide-eyed and giddy looks we were shooting at each other across the orchestra.

Well, I guess we *were* up to something.

CHAPTER 7

The Great Sell-off

OCTOBER 2019

W E LET OUR FAMILY and out-of-town friends know the news immediately. We were selling everything and leaving the country on November 18. But our workplace was another thing, and we thought a lot about how, when, and to whom we should tender our resignations.

October rolled around, and the day came to let our employers know. We did so bluntly. "We got visas to work in Italy, so we're quitting next month to move there." The responses were interesting — less surprised at the Italy element, more surprised at the fact that we were doing it at our age, and especially surprised that we were giving up our jobs. In the orchestra business, positions such as ours are extremely difficult to obtain. Quitting almost certainly meant we were giving up orchestra life permanently.

We had good working relationships with many of our colleagues, and they were happy for us, if sad to hear we'd be leaving. But we knew more than a few who felt differently: Two decades of boundary-pushing, status-quo-challenging, and general boat-rocking hadn't exactly put us on the top of everyone's Christmas card lists.

One of our managers had a cleareyed response. She was not surprised at our decision, having watched us do "this travel thing" for years — writing guidebooks, starting a consulting business. "It was just a matter of time before you guys would figure a way to do this."

Yes, we're really lucky, we agreed.

"No, there's no luck," she said, as if quoting an aphorism.

"It's just preparation meeting opportunity." That phrase has stuck with us ever since.

Meanwhile, we cranked into overdrive with our big "Stuff Sell-off." Every day, we listed 10 or 15 items for sale: a desk chair, candlesticks, shelves, tools, a TV, a lawnmower. You name it, we were selling it. I fielded dozens of messages every day, managing pickups of "merchandise." It seemed like we were running a K-Mart, albeit with fewer workers and no in-store security.

And of course we had to do all this while still continuing to do our jobs — practicing and rehearsing and performing several concerts a week, recording, and all the rest, while trying to keep my white tie and vest from getting too yellow. We had worked out our schedule so that our final concert with the orchestra, just a week before we'd be leaving, was with a guest conductor, performing Berlioz's *Symphony Fantastique* — about as spectacular a sendoff as we could hope for.

At the same time, we had to keep the house as clean as possible, since our Realtor was organizing house showings. For each of these, before we evacuated the house, we had to sequester all four cats in a little office upstairs. Prospective buyers had to open the door and peek into the office to see it without crossing the baby gate we had set up and without letting the litterboxes inside detract from their interest in the house. Again, it wasn't the ideal house-showing situation, but it was what circumstances allowed. You want to know what's totally relaxing? Keeping a house spotless and showroom-ready while working full-time, while four cats do their damnedest to filth things up, then inviting a dozen people into your house each day to buy random stuff.

That last bit actually helped though, and the showings gradually got easier, as our possessions slowly dwindled. We saved some of our more meaningful possessions to give to particular friends or family: a handmade wooden bench to a friend for her house in the woods; stacks and stacks of sheet music to various colleagues and students; antique glassware to a friend who hosted cocktail parties.

Our kitchen was particularly well-equipped. Zen loved cooking, and we hosted dinner parties a few times each month. We didn't sell any of that stuff, though. Instead, we arranged to donate it all to a local organization that helped people who were experiencing homelessness. They were just finishing a project creating about a dozen tiny homes, and our kitchen stuff could outfit several of them.

Zeneba had made a stack of lists on yellow legal pads — every category had its own pad. Cat transport, packing, instruments, medical visits — the logistics seemed endless. Every task needed to be carefully considered and planned and timed.

There were lists for emotional things, too — last dinners or drinks with special friends, giving certain prized items to the right people. We also hoped to have a goodbye party, which we wanted to be a Big Deal. We had hosted countless dinners and cocktail parties in this house over the years — dinners with friends, meetings with board members, and dinners for donors to the chamber ensemble we directed, holiday cocktail parties... So one last gathering seemed in order — if we could organize it along with everything else that needed doing.

Since we didn't know what to expect from our new life in Italy, we made a point of visiting our doctors and dentist to get a final checkup and to collect our records. We scheduled exams for every possible procedure, involving pretty much every orifice. Though the US systems of healthcare are demonstrably not as good as those in Italy, we wanted to put off for as long as possible the need to explain any orifice-related issues in a foreign language.

Our cats, too, needed full examinations — their medical papers needed to be perfectly in order to be accepted into Italy. We took all four of them to our veterinary clinic at the same time, for bloodwork, microchip insertion, and vaccinations. Despite our unfortunately broad experience with trips to the vet, taking in all of them at once was a new challenge of controlled chaos — the meowing and hissing and struggling to get into (or out of) a carrier, multiplied fourfold. (We explained to the cats that this was nothing compared to the transatlantic voyage they were about to endure, but despite our years of tutelage, their English comprehension is limited to "Get down" and "Go do something else somewhere else.")

Our vet gave us folders full of medical records for each of the cats. Mr. Weasely's was inches thick. Over the years, we had spent a ton of money (as well as emotional currency) on a hellish array of procedures to treat his various maladies. We had moved heaven and earth to keep him alive and healthy and happy. He had three different veterinary pharmacies, a hematologist, an ophthalmologist (yes, that's a thing), and two allergists, and he had undergone multiple serious surgeries. Through it all, Weasely took it all like a champ, taking his medicines and procedures and special food preparations, and meanwhile playing fetch when we were bored (he retrieved little spongy balls, like a dog) and snuggling up to Zen or me when one of us was sick or stressed. He would lie with us for hours at a time, transforming into a boneless bag of hot sand and purring like a lawnmower. He was an old cat at this point, and we had decided a couple of years earlier that we wouldn't put him through any more major traumatic procedures.

The cats were getting anxious at the flurry of activity, especially when one of their preferred chairs or rugs or pillows was literally sold out from underneath them. Except for Weasely — as ever, his empathetic soul saw our stress, and he put his own concerns aside to console us.

Now that we had sorted the logistical challenge of the cats' paperwork, we turned to another: packing, and getting to the Atlanta airport on November 18th. Despite getting rid of probably 95 percent of what we owned, for our "final" trip we were still taking a *lot* of stuff: the cats, some personal items and clothes, computers, and two instruments — including my cello, which is Not Small. The cello and Zen's violin were the most valuable thing we owned, and these instruments are fragile and sensitive. You can't put a cello underneath a plane like checked baggage without serious risk of damage. In many cases, to do so would invalidate the insurance coverage. It would be like putting a piece of Louis XV furniture in a duffel bag and tossing it in with the rest of the luggage.

Between moving the cello and the cats, we had looked into every possibility. Sailing over with the cats on the QE2. Shipping the instruments with a company used by diplomats, or shipping them to a luthier's shop in Italy. Asking some US orchestra going on a European tour to do us a favor and take the cello with them and drop it somewhere that we could drive to pick it up. Buying plane tickets for friends and having them fly over with us — everyone gets a cat as a carry-on! Buying a seat for the cello on the plane.

Yet another challenge: We had a Honda Element to get rid of, somehow. Abandoning it in a parking garage in Atlanta to be discovered months later by police seemed like not the best option. (But it was *an* option.) And worse: As Zen enumerated the things we needed to get to Atlanta — every cat carrier, suitcase, instrument case — I crawled into the back of the car with a tape measure to scope out the interior. I could feel the gears of my brain grinding and crunching as I realized there was not enough space for everything. I gave the bad news to Zen.

"Okay, fan-f***ing-tastic," Zen chirped. "I wish we had time to f***ing figure this out, but we have to f***ing get dressed for the f***ing Beethoven concert a f***ing hour from now. (It was moments like this, by the way, that made us think that our neigh-bors with small children were probably not really sorry that we were moving.)

We had really hit a wall. As we got ready for the concert, we posed possible solutions for each challenge, discarding each one in turn as we realized it wasn't feasible. We could practically hear the game show "BZZZZZT!" buzzing as each option fell by the wayside for one reason or another. Zen took a few precious min-utes to post about our challenges on social media, asking for a solution and presenting our issues to a sizeable brain trust — the combined intellect and creativity of all of our friends online.

Ten minutes after she posted this, as we were about to head out the door, the phone rang. It was my cousin. She had already been thinking about visiting us in Nashville a few days ahead of our departure. "I saw your post. We'll buy your car from you!" she said with her characteristic irrepressible cheer. "My son needs a vehicle for school — it would be perfect." I just about cried. She would be in Atlanta for a while visiting her daughter, so the timing worked out well.

She came up to Nashville a couple of days later, helped us pack some things, and left with two big suitcases that we'd be taking with us overseas. This freed up vital space in our Honda for our own trip to Atlanta a few days later.

One problem we had not yet resolved was how to manage another of our cats, Socksie. Though she was a sweetheart to us, she was something of an instigator with the three boys. Once or twice in years past, her fights with Mr. Weasely, in particular, had gotten so bad that we needed to take both of them in for what our veterinarian called "couple's counseling." This amounted to careful monitoring and sequestering and reintro-ductions — and sedatives. (Pharmaceuticals for the cats, wine for us.) We imagined that taking all four of these animals to a tiny single-room place after a 24-hour ordeal in an airplane cargo hold would be tantamount to yelling "Fire" in the proverbial crowded theater — if the theater was filled with two dozen flesh-hungry zombies. This problem — along with the rest of our logistical challenges — kept us up at night.

One evening, just a week before we were scheduled to leave, our friend Sandy was at our house to pick up the aforementioned big wooden bench. Artfully made from mountain laurel wood, this was one of the first "crafty" gifts we had bought for the house in our first year of marriage, found at a rural artisan workshop in the Blue Ridge Mountains, and it was meaningful to us that our friend was taking it. Sandy is a cat-mom and general animal lover, and her "treehouse" in the country is a literal wildlife refuge where our rustic bench would fit in perfectly.

As we stood chatting with her in our now nearly empty living room, we told her of our anxiety about Socksie. "I'll take her for a while, if that would help," she offered. "A few weeks or whatever."

It felt like a huge blessing. We almost wept as Zen and I both leapt on the idea. We could buy Sandy a plane ticket to bring Socksie over in January, and pick up her lodging and meal expenses, too.

"That's crazy," she objected. "That would be so expensive, you guys." Indeed it would, but we explained that we had already considered every possible scenario for doing all of this. Moving just three cats was already costing a bundle. Paying her way to Italy would be just another in the array of huge expenses. And, as a bonus, we'd get to see our dear friend again. It was a win-win, and a massive weight off our shoulders. By the time Socksie arrived in January, we figured, Weasely and the other two boys would have become well-adjusted to the space, and Socksie could fold right in — perhaps with the help of some of those prescriptions we talked about.

Sandy came back a few days later to collect Socksie and some of her stuff, among which was a fancy orthopedic pillow that Zen had bought (per her chiropractor's advice) to help with some neck problems. Cat owners will not be surprised to learn that Socksie had gradually claimed the pillow as decidedly "hers," so it was going with her to Sandy's house.

Socksie meowed and whined as we put her into her carrier and into Sandy's car. We said goodbye to both of them. Though we had plans to reunite with Socksie, we also recognized that we were venturing into so much uncertainty with our new lives, and... well, you never know. It was a terribly emotional moment for everyone concerned — and we felt the most for Socksie, who of course couldn't understand why we seemed to be abandoning her. As Sandy drove away, there were tears all around.

We had worked out our last days with the symphony to conclude a week before we left the country, so we'd have some breathing room in our schedule to get everything else done. We were performing the famous *Symphonie Fantastique* by Berlioz, a huge and fascinating piece. It was one of those pieces that, although we had played it countless times since our teenage years, didn't feel overplayed like so much of the standard orchestral repertoire can. And the guest conductor was someone we really enjoyed working with. (It should be noted that for an orchestra musician to say that they like *any* conductor is quite a rare thing.)

It's typical, upon the retirement of an orchestra musician, for the management to do a little presentation to the audience at their last concert: "Here's so-and-so who has played with the Symphony for this many years; we want to take the time to acknowledge their indispensable contributions to the organization and so on and so forth; please give them a big round of applause to show our *et cetera et cetera*." But we had explicitly asked our management not to do this. We wanted to go out quietly. Over our careers in Nashville, we had received plenty of recognition in other arenas, including reviews and accolades in the newspapers (remember newspapers?) for our concerts and recordings and other activities with our group ALIAS Chamber Ensemble, as well as write-ups as "local authors" when we published our guidebooks. In fact we had even written *for* the paper, having published several travel articles for local and national outlets. So we didn't feel like we needed or wanted any special recognition from the symphony, and they were happy to respect our wishes.

A lot of thoughts were swirling in our heads during this last concert. As we often did, we looked out at the audience while we played. We made eye contact with a lot of patrons who we had gotten to know over the years. Many of them were donors to our ensemble as well, and had been in our home, dining and sampling our Italian *liquori* collection.

Berlioz's *Fantastique* is famous in part for his use of the Dies Irae, an ancient chant melody associated with death. As we played the notes of this ominous tune, we were conflicted. Was this the end of our careers? Would this be the last time we played in a symphony orchestra? We didn't know, but we tried to just dive into the music. The orchestra hall in Nashville is a spectacular place, with a near-perfect acoustic that allows the sounds of the instruments to wash over musicians and audience alike. When we played the final notes of the piece, the audience erupted in applause, which itself overwhelmed us — that great acoustic works both ways. As the guest conductor beckoned the orchestra to stand up (he declined to take his own personal bow), the sound of 3,000 hands clapping crashed over us like a tidal wave. Afterward, we said some farewells to a few choice colleagues, packed our instruments, and walked out of the hall to our scooters for the last time.

After many weeks of unloading our stuff onto our community, we had accumulated a nice little stash of cash. We decided that a good use for this would be to hold a fantastic goodbye party for our best friends and colleagues. Lots of beer and wine, and catered by a local Syrian restaurant that we loved. The "street value" of all of our life's accumulated stuff, it turns out, buys a lot of hummus! The restaurant had to bring their own tables, though. By the time the party rolled around, ours were all gone. Indeed, the only piece of furniture left in the house was our bed. We had sold all the lamps, and we had long ago removed two big overhead electric light fixtures and replaced them with "candeliers," so the entire house was lit only by candles. A pair of shipping boxes that would be picked up the next day to be sent to Italy ahead of us served as cocktail tables, and by the end of the night they were covered with wax and wine stains.

The party was a wonderful gathering of people from all walks of Nashville life: Musicians, of course, but also journalists, medical professionals, photographers, activists and writers and restauranteurs and shop owners and... It was heartwarming to see that, in addition to all the stuff, we had been fortunate to accumulate so many interesting and diverse friends over the 20 years we lived and worked in Nashville.

Upon entering, all of our friends read a sign that we had put on the front door: No One Is Permitted to Leave Without Taking Something From The Table. We had set up a table by the door with a wide array of stuff — the handful of things we had yet to sell, donate, or throw away. Some were valuable or meaningful: books, fancy glassware, candles, bottles of *liquori* that we couldn't finish (as hard as we tried!). Others were just useful — a pack of napkins, a roll of aluminum foil, an inkjet printer, some light-bulbs. One of our guests — the director of Nashville's opera company — picked up a big straw animal. This was Zen's Julbok, a traditional yule-goat, common to Swedish Christmas festivities. "Can I really have this?" he asked. "I'll put it on stage for *Amahl and the Night Visitors* coming up next month."

A great many of our friends offered emotional goodbyes to our cats as well as to us — Mr. Weasely and Hoover, especially, were minor celebrities in town, and everybody loved them. Some of them had been our cat-sitters over the years, in fact, so they knew these individual cat personalities intimately.

In our last few days, Zeneba's parents came to town, offering more help with the rest of the packing and selling and disposing of stuff. They agreed to take a box of our memorabilia, thereby deferring some difficult decisions. Unfortunately, we had already made some of those decisions — discarding Zen's high school yearbook and boxes of notes she had saved from third grade through senior year, among other things. She even got rid of her wedding dress. It was hopelessly stained with wine (naturally) but of course it was still meaningful. She did save a scrap of it to bring with us. This was emblematic of what we had been doing on a larger scale — retaining just the smallest portions of the stories of our old lives, to embark on a new chapter.

Two days before we left, Zen's parents went with us to the local NPR classical station, for our final performance in the States. We were broadcasting live on the radio, for an audience that spanned across the state. We had done many of these over the years, and they were unusual experiences, because they amounted to "one-take" recordings. We questioned our sanity at putting ourselves through this less than 48 hours before we left, but we wanted our last musical event to be just the two of us. We played a piece of Italian Baroque music and a blues duo piece that I had written a few years ago. The mix of Italian and American seemed fitting.

It was yet another bittersweet event — a sort of final musical goodbye to the life we had built in Nashville and its music industry.

The next day — one day before we were to leave — Zen woke up with a 102-degree fever. Normally in this circumstance, I'd go to the store and get the makings for chicken soup. Now that all of our stuff was gone, that was impossible. Instead, between chores (because things still needed doing), she pounded Dayquil and orange juice and vitamin C tablets, and we got a delivery of some Thai soup and other spicy dishes. It was the best we could do, and Zen soldiered on. Her fever broke, but she was still feeling crappy all day.

We did get a bit of good news, though: Our Realtor called and said there was an offer on the house, so he was getting that ball rolling and collecting some "earnest money" from the buyer. That was a huge relief, as our plan depended on the house being sold in the very near future.

On "The Day," when we left the house for good, we had imagined a poignant scene like the final episode of a sit-com. Instead, and predictably, it was a mad, desperate scramble. As hard as we had tried, we hadn't quite managed to get rid of everything. We spent a few frantic minutes cleaning up a few messes — one of the cats chose that morning to barf in the kitchen one final time and, having gotten rid really of almost everything, we had to improvise to clean it up. Things still remained in our shed outside, and our bed was supposed to be picked up later that same day. (Spoiler: The buyers blew it off and our Realtor had to pay a guy to haul it away. We had reimbursed him for this — one last *ka-ching!*)

Ultimately, this is what the drive to Atlanta airport looked like: several suitcases, three cat carriers, a violin case, two computer bags, and a cello in a huge, coffin-like case specially designed so it could fly in cargo... and did we mention the worm farm?

You read that right. Among the things that my cousin was going to take with her on her visit — was *excited* to take, in fact — was a vermicomposter that we had in our back yard. Unfortunately, in all the chaos, we had neglected to load it up into her car; so we had to haul it down to Atlanta along with everything else. These couple hundred worms had lived with us for the past 10 years or so. And while we hadn't exactly named them (not all of them, anyway), they were sort of pets, too.

About an hour into the drive to Atlanta, Zen was flipping through our "cat papers."

"Ohhh... Ummm..." she said in that voice that people use when things are Not Exactly Okay. "These are Hoover's original adoption papers, and they list him as a 'white-and-black' cat."

Crap. Hoover, our youngest cat, had come to us when he was a young kitten. He is all white now; but as a kitten he had a black patch on his head, which faded over the years. We wanted everything regarding the cats to be logistically perfect. What if some Customs official sees those papers and says "This is not the same cat, this one's all white!"

Zen checked her map app and said "Take this next exit, there's a Walgreens." When we got there, Zen dashed in and came out a few minutes later with a little bag.

"Mascara," she said. "Not tested on animals. Let's start now." We got Hoover out of his carrier and I held him while she applied the stuff to the top of his head. It looked pretty convincing.

We proceeded to the cargo area of the airport. Here we met the pet shipper, who had brought us two massive, international travel crates, as well as the reams of paperwork required to shuffle the cats through customs. We moved Hoover and Coconut into their crates to be stowed under the plane. This was scary, too. Although we had every expectation that they'd be fine (albeit stressed), we had to sign papers to the effect that we understood that Bad Things Can Happen. But it was the only way. We said a last "Attaboy" to the two of them, then we left.

My cousin met us in a long-term parking lot. We switched things between the vehicles (she took the worms!), then she drove us to the Departures section of the airport. I had to grab not one but two luggage carts to carry all of our stuff: five big suitcases, a duffel bag, computer bags, Zen's violin, my giant cello case, and Mr. Weasely in his soft carrier. It seemed ridiculous, not least because of the size of the home we were going to.

The first stop inside was the oversized baggage office, where I dropped off my cello. The security people there made me unpack the whole thing — taking the regular case out of the big rubber coffin-case, then taking out the cello. I gave them a little 30-second concert, demonstrating the instrument and its parts, and showed them my various ownership documents, before packing it all up again and receiving a baggage claim ticket. They wheeled it away and, as with every step of this process, I hoped for the best.

At the check-in counter we were paying through the nose for our extra bags, a few of which were overweight, as well. The airline clerk was extremely helpful with our long and complicated check-in process, weighing each bag and advising us how to rearrange the things in them to make at least one of the bags come in underweight. We chatted with her while we scrambled with the bags. We introduced her to Weasely, of course, and she instantly loved him.

"I can waive the extra fee for that fifth bag," the clerk whispered conspiratorially. I was floored. With a few clicks of her keyboard, she had just saved us a few hundred bucks. Overwhelmed almost to tears with gratitude, Zen rooted through our stuff to come up with a suitable gift as a thank-you. We settled on one of my belts (I had only two), handmade with ostrich leather, that we'd bought in Tuscany. It would be perfect for her fiancé, about whom we had learned while waiting for the computer to process our flight information.

"Here's our card," Zen said, "and I wrote the name of the town where we got it, in case you ever get to Italy and want to visit there." The clerk seemed moved by the gesture, strange though it was. This moving process required us to give away so many of our treasured items. In many cases, the giving of them was more meaningful than the possessing of them had ever been.

We stopped at a bar in the terminal for a cocktail to calm our nerves. Weasely's carrier had little fold-out netted extensions so he could feel a little less cramped. People walking by stopped to meet him and marvel at what an adorable picture he made — a big cottonball lounging in what looked like a little pop-out camper. The flight attendants, too, cooed over him as we boarded the plane. He was making friends everywhere, as always — now internationally.

The flight itself was uneventful — a haze of fretting and fitful sleep. Every bump made me wonder how our other two cats were doing. Near the end of the flight, some turbulence jostled the plane quite a bit. Typically in these moments Zen would hold my hand, assuaging my fear of flying. (No, it's a fear of *crashing*, I always hasten to clarify.) But in this instance her attention was occupied, as Weasel had pissed himself and also vomited a little. We had come prepared for such an occurrence: Puppy pee pads, wipes, sanitizers. But there was only so much we could do, and Zen got pretty damp. We experienced a moment of sympathy for what it must be like to travel with a baby.

"I also get to enjoy the rest of my day smelling like a litter box," Zen added.

Luckily we landed shortly thereafter and walked through passport control with no problems. We queued in a different line from the one we usually used when we were visiting — this one was for holders of visas. That was us!

As we approached baggage claim, a woman came up to us wheeling my cello on a cart. She checked it against my ticket, and then held up a finger and reached for her phone.

"*Aspetta*," she said, distracted. Wait? For what? We held our breath — then she held up her phone and showed us pictures. "*Ecco vostri gatti*," she said, smiling. She had pictures of our Hoover and Coconut, unloaded in their crates safe and sound!

We thanked her profusely. She waved it off. "*Adoro tutti gatti*," she explained — I love all cats. Now all we had to do was collect them at the customs cargo area of the airport.

We eventually got our bags from the carousel — all five — and loaded everything up on two trolleys. I fingered the computer bag, ready to instantly produce Mr. Weasely's paperwork and anything else the security officers needed. But they were busy talking to one another, giving us only the slightest glance before we walked on through.

A short, familiar hike got us to the rental car area. Again Mr. Weasely was a big star here among all those waiting to sort out their cars. We had rented two, in this case — one for just one day, and the other for a few weeks. Zen would drive what turned out to be a minivan. We did need the space, but she was apprehensive about it: She had not driven in Europe in our 14 years of overseas travels. She had barely driven our car in the US for several years. To say she was out of practice was an understatement.

Nevertheless, we loaded everything into these two cars, and headed to the customs area, a couple of miles from the passenger terminals. Even though our paperwork was 100 percent in order, picking up our other two cats proved much more complicated than we anticipated. We left my rental outside of the security area, with our instruments in it. Trying to blend in and be fully Italian, I parked creatively in an illegal space, thinking this was a 10-minute endeavor. It turned out to be nearly two hours, and it felt like about 17. So in addition to stinking like cat piss, we also reeked of flop sweat, worrying that the car was going to be towed, and we'd get deported for breaking the law on Day One.

The customs cargo area is a huge acreage covered by a bunch of grim, soulless gray offices and warehouses and loading docks. After gaining secured entry into the area, we went from office to office, getting varied instructions to other offices for stamps and signatures from different people, in separate departments and buildings. A couple of times we inadvertently exited the security area and had to wait while they re-authorized our re-entry. The whole ordeal would almost have been funny, if we weren't in a total panic thinking that Hoover and Coconut were literally shitting themselves in their cages while they waited, not to mention the fear that our rental car and our instruments would be seized or stolen and we would have no means to support ourselves after we'd just quit our jobs and sold everything we own.

Eventually we got every necessary document, stamp, and signature, and we waited for another... three hours? (actual time: about 10 minutes more) at a giant warehouse door. At last, a guy pushing a pallet-jack came driving through the door with a pile of containers — led by none other than our two boys in their crates! They had also pissed themselves at some point during the whole ordeal, but otherwise they looked fine, and Coconut even seemed happy to see us. (He's usually not happy to see anyone.)

After we loaded them into the minivan and returned to where I had parked the other car, we discovered that a bunch of other people had taken my lead, creating their own spaces behind mine.

"See?" Zen said, pointing. "We can be leaders in our community."

"Hahaha," I replied, "Let's get the hell out of here."

The drive to Soriano was unremarkable — at least for me, carrying just the instruments and bags. For Zen in the minivan with the cats, it was a different story.

"This was not exactly" she said — after sleeping for maybe two hours (15 minutes at a time), treating herself to a breakfast of a double espresso and two DayQuils, driving in rain, with drivers honking when she stalled out at the toll booth because she hadn't driven a car in like 10 years, all the while sitting in the lingering cloud of cat urine and listening to the incessant mewing from all three boys from their containers for the whole drive — "the makings of a beautiful day."

But we got there. We backed down the driveway and unloaded everything, the cats last of all. I put out their water and food in the kitchen, and prepped the litterboxes upstairs. We set down their carriers in the living room and opened them up. They came out sniffing, cautious, suspicious.

We had done it. Zen called to them in a sing-songy voice:

"Welcome home, kittens!"

CHAPTER 8

Dark Days

WINTER 2019

*B*ACK IN AUGUST, Zeneba had planted a bunch of pansy seeds in the flower box in our front window — another "gift" from the previous owner. When we arrived in November, we were shocked to see that box bursting with pansies. How could this be possible, that those seeds sprouted and flourished with only rainwater to nourish them?

Of course it wasn't possible, we soon learned. Our neighbor Giuseppina had planted new flowers as a welcome gesture. We were (and indeed we remain) so grateful to our neighbors for their kindness and welcoming generosity.

Right out of the gate, we had a rehearsal lined up: Some mutual connections led us to be invited to play with an amateur Baroque ensemble, and there would be a rehearsal just a few days after our arrival. One of its members was Floriana, a soprano who lived here in Soriano, and we had contacted her to ask her if she might print the music for us, as we didn't know when we'd have that capability. She dropped the music off at a local shop, along with a gift of a bottle of wine and a pair of the biggest wine glasses we'd ever seen. Another lovely welcome, from someone who would quickly become a treasured friend here in Soriano.

Although we had done a fair job over the summer of preparing this apartment to be lived in, we still needed to sort out a lot of things, including finding space for the contents of the bags we had carried with us on the flight over. Among the items that were the most important to us was a pair of paintings by Zen's Uncle John — two idyllic and fantastical images of Vermont. Our friend Lee, knowledgeable in such things, had helped us detach them from their frames, roll them up, and put them, protected, into one of our suitcases. (She had also given us the suitcase!) Having arrived in Italy, we took them to a well-regarded art shop in Viterbo; but the folks there refused to frame the paintings, for fear of damaging them. So our next stop, after I carefully measured the paintings to the millimeter (yes, I had since bought a metric tape-measure), was the Brico store, the Italian equivalent of a Home Depot. I gave my exact measurements to the guys in the lumber department, explaining that I needed to construct *due cornice,* and they cut me pieces of wood that I could use to build the two frames. I got some hardware (screws, brackets), drove home, and set to work on our living room floor, carefully assembling and affixing to the best of my ability.

This kind of thing is not really my strong suit. "If this actually works, I want a shitload of points," I told Zen.

"You'll do a great job — you're so smart and good at this," she replied. She knew the result would be better with some encouragement, despite what we both know is my distinctly amateur skill with such jobs.

In the end, though, my primitive framing worked reasonably well, and I did indeed get my shitload of points. So now Uncle John's paintings hang prominently — and only ever so slightly crookedly — in our little Italian home.

We returned the minivan the day after we arrived, but we had the other rental car for a few weeks, so we set about getting as much done as we could. Stocking up on heavier items — cases of canned tomatoes, bottles of various things, bags of pellets for heating (and for cat-peeing!). Bags of pellets were 15 kg each — about 33 pounds — so that was *not* something we wanted to have to schlep one bag at a time from the *piazza.*

We also had business to attend to. Two days after we arrived, we drove up to Firenze for a meeting with our *avvocato.* Shortly after we had engaged him, he was interviewed by *CBS Sunday Morning* and then by PBS, due to his expertise in Italian immigration law, so we felt great about having him handle our paperwork.

Within eight days of arriving in the country, we were required to submit our paperwork for our *Permesso di Soggiorno* — the permit to stay in the country. This is what seems to us like a ton of impenetrable paperwork: lots of taxes and fees to pay, submitted at the post office in a particular way. Many people do this part themselves, but we wanted our lawyer's help. We had put so much on the table, trading away security (our salaried orchestra job), space (selling our big home to live in a tiny one), and comfort (selling or giving away so many material things). In exchange, we received time and heart — that is, getting to move to Italy at this point in our lives and live our dream. And we weren't willing to risk all of that for the sake of saving a few bucks. Throughout this process we had engaged (and placed our trust in) the expertise of professionals, and our *avvocato* is a prime example.

At his office, he filled out our paperwork, then literally walked with us to the post office. Watching the whole process, we feel more confident that in a year or two we will be able to do this on our own. But for the time being, *vale la pena* — it's worth the penalty.

As expected, the drive and the process took a good bit of the day, so we had arranged to stay at a little B&B in Pienza on the way back. This has always been one of our favorite towns to visit. Its view of the Val d'Orcia from the town's "balcony" walkway is stunning, with Monte Amiata looming in the distance.

"Hey Matto," Zen said quietly as we looked at that view, which we had seen countless times over the years. "Do you think about the fact that beyond that mountain is our little town, and our own little house?"

"And our cats are there too, waiting for us!" I added, grinning.

We were clearly still deep in the "I can't believe it" stage of this move.

A few days later, we drove across the Tiber valley to attend our first gathering of the baroque group, who had invited us to join them for a concert in December. Floriana agreed to lead us in her big family minivan, and we followed in our little rental. We struggled to keep up with her car as she breezed along the little country roads to the rehearsal location.

It was a social bunch, a mix of at least five nationalities and even more professions. Most of them spoke at least some English, though we did our best to discuss as much as possible in Italian. (It helps that most of the standard classical music vocabulary we've been steeped in since childhood is Italian, so this was not a huge stretch.) Zen's stand partner was an Englishwoman who had lived in Italy for some 15 years. In contrast to her previous stand partner (who was not Zen's biggest fan, to say the least), Lois was welcoming, lighthearted and collegial. I could see that they were hitting it off right away, cracking little wry jokes to one another. (After nearly 30 years playing in professional symphonies, I had become adept in reading body language across the orchestra, and especially Zen's, of course. I can see instantly when she enjoys her stand partner — and when she doesn't — and I can practically transcribe the joke she's making based on her facial expression.)

The rehearsal, too, stood in stark contrast to what we had grown accustomed to over the past two decades. In a professional union-contract orchestra in the States, start/stop times and breaks are rigorously timed, down to the second. Here, as with the small chamber group that we ran in the US, it was much more informal. Each *pausa* was a lengthy break for everyone to chat and eat and drink. It was an invigorating introduction to at least one facet of the musical scene in our new home.

Having met — and now having made music with — Floriana, we asked her to help us organize a little concert at a retirement home in Soriano for Christmas. She happened to have a contact at the Residenza just up the street from our house, so she agreed to reach out and set it up. Community service was always a large part of our activity in Nashville, with our chamber ensemble and on our own, and we wanted to do the same in our new community. And with the holiday season around the corner, this seemed like a good way to start.

Thanksgiving rolled around. This is not a holiday in Italy, of course. A day when family gets together and reflects on gratitude and eats a lot of food, is just called Thursday here.

Try as we might, we were unable to find a whole turkey for sale anywhere. We asked at a local butcher. We explained to him that Thanksgiving is a special day in the States.

He was familiar with it. "*Si, quando i tacchini sono molto arrabbiati,*" he said — It's when the turkeys are very angry! In any case, he had no whole turkeys. We would have had to special-order it weeks ahead of time. But he did have a turkey breast. So we cooked an *involtini,* rolled up with vegetables and herbs, and roasted. It was a nice nod to American traditions while being immersed in our new Italian life.

The next evening, we got a call from our Realtor. "I didn't want to bother you on the holiday," he said. "But the buyer had problems with financing, and the house sale fell through."

This was a harsh blow. Our whole situation here in Italy depended, in large part, on selling that house in a reasonably short period of time. We had moved with a little cushion in place, since our work in Italy wouldn't really crank up until the new year, and our overhead now was minimal — no rent or mortgage, affordable food, cheap utilities. But we really needed the house to sell. This felt like more than a hitch, and it placed a giant concrete question mark on our backs.

Our Realtor assured us he'd do his best to get it sold as soon as possible, and he was confident, but the uncertainty of it all was almost unbearable. It was highly unusual for Americans to move here to work, especially self-employed. We didn't love that in our first week out of the gate, it looked like we were already broke.

But there was nothing to do but wait. As our Realtor had told us, "You guys sitting there worrying isn't going to make this house sell any faster. Just do your thing, and I'll do my thing, and we'll hope for the best."

He was right, of course.

Despite the setback, we wanted to project an image that we were successful and capable and that everything was going according to plan. And we still had a paid-for rental car, and we still needed to run errands and so on. So in the subsequent days we started taking daily excursions to the surrounding towns and points of interest in our area. These trips were practically free — it costs nothing to wander medieval streets and admire the artwork in Renaissance churches.

As December rolled in and the days began to get shorter, each town had *Natale* (Christmas) decorations going up in its *piazza*. One day we visited the town on the other side of our Cimino mountain, Canepina, historically famous for the production of hemp (*canapa*). Their Christmas tree in the square was decked with dozens of red Santa hats. Here we bought a *panettone*, a traditional holiday cake. This one was unique to the town, made with hemp and chocolate chips.

Another day took us to the ancient town of Vitorchiano, which is watched over by a giant Moai statue, carved from local stone some 30 years ago by visitors from Easter Island. The narrow streets within its medieval walls were decorated with a series of *Presepe*, ornately crafted nativity scenes.

Next door to Soriano we found the little town of Bassano in Teverina. A huge Christmas tree sat in the middle of its tiny town square, in front of a 12th-century church. In an adjacent building, a vending machine dispenses wine for €1.50 per liter — just insert your *tessera sanitaria* (the national health card) and put your empty bottle under the dispenser. With each visit, every new discovery, we remarked on how lucky we were to have found a home so close to dozens of such fascinating locations. (And not just because of the wine machine.)

All of these adorable holiday decorations put us in a festive mood, so of course we went to get our own tree for our house. In Nashville, we'd get a big Douglas fir, the biggest one we could fit in our house, and we decked out the whole house with several large boxes of straw ornaments and lights. We held a holiday party every year for about 150 people involved with our chamber ensemble — patrons, board members, volunteers, musicians — and we made all the food ourselves. It was a huge operation that took weeks of preparation.

In our new place, it was hard to figure out where to even put a tree, and it would have to be a tiny one. All of our ornaments fit into a shoebox now, and it takes about 25 minutes to decorate everything. We got a tree at a *vivaio* (plant nursery), a live tree in its own little pot. It was perfect for our little home, and later we'd give it to someone who could replant it somewhere, so it could keep growing.

The result was a micro-version of the holiday scene in our home in Nashville — our decorations (about 5 percent of them, anyway), our cats, our candles on the tree.

As previously mentioned, we have always been cheapskates — that was one of the factors that enabled us to move here in the first place. But now, with the uncertainty of the house hanging over us, we became even more mindful of spending. A local friend asked us to join her for a ballet concert in Viterbo, and another invited us to a fancy New Year's Eve party at a local restaurant — something that normally we'd have been glad to do. Now we felt a need to defer such things until we had a clearer picture of our situation.

But we kept up these little "free tours," at least, until a week before Christmas, when we had to return the car.

That same day, the thing that we had been dreading for years finally happened.

Our beloved Mr. Weasely was feeling ill. We had long ago learned the signs of his various maladies — his voice, behavior, body language, litter box issues, even his facial expressions. He'd practically tell us that something was wrong. And so he did this day.

I had to return our rental car, so while I drove to Viterbo, Zen carried him to the vet clinic, just a few minutes' walk down the hill from our place — we had driven by it dozens of times. It was a tiny shop with a little exam room in the back, and the patients sometimes included goats as well as dogs and cats.

The doctor took one look at Weasel and then yelled at the other people waiting — something to the effect that they needed to get out of the way so he could deal with our animal. *"Subito!"* he yelled — Right away! The doc didn't speak a word of English, but his vet technician had a few key words, and with Zen's Italian she could communicate with her effectively enough.

I had dropped off the car and was waiting for a friend with whom I had arranged to get back to Soriano. But my ride was running late, so I had nothing to do but wait powerlessly and exchange messages and calls with Zen, as she updated me through heaving sobs on what the doc was saying and what she could glean from some spur-of-the-moment online reading. Weasely was severely anemic, and he might have major kidney and/or liver failure. The doc had set him up with IV fluids and put him in a crate for observation.

This was potentially an end-of-life situation.

Minutes seemed like hours. I finally made my way back to Soriano and found Zen sitting alone in a little green-space park next to the clinic. We sat there for a few minutes, hugging and crying a lot. I wondered if people walking by recognized the look of someone dealing with the pain of a pet in distress.

After we collected ourselves a bit, we went back into the clinic, and Zen introduced me to the vet and his tech.

The doc cut straight to the chase: Signor Weasely's best bet, he explained, was if he could get a blood transfusion.

Is that a thing here, a blood bank for cats? We had never heard of such a thing in the US.

"No," he answered, *"abbiamo bisogno di un gatto grosso per donare."* You'd need a big healthy cat to use as a donor. Do you know one? It seemed crazy, but yes, we did. I walked back to our house and shuffled Hoover into a carrier and brought him to the clinic.

Things work differently in a small-town clinic in Italy than they would in the States. Here, we were invited back to the exam room to be with our cat, while the doc and his tech went from one case to the next, seeing to his other patients one by one. When it came to getting blood from Hoover, guess who was helping the doc? Not the vet tech — she was busy.

It was surreal. He and I proceeded to extract blood from Hoover's neck, one vacuum vial at a time. As I held him Hoover protested mightily, while the doc tried to soothe him: *"Bravo Hoover, che eroe."* What a hero, Hoover.

Luckily, since we had pared down our lives to a sliver of what they once were, we were able to move around other appointments to be totally free this day and the next.

Zen was comforting Weasely, who watched his little friend struggling against the manhandling and blood extraction. Zen and I were both choking back tears at the trauma of it all. Eventually we got the number of vials the doc wanted. The tech bandaged up Hoover and put him in his carrier to wait and watch.

The next task was to put the blood into Weasel's IV. And guess whose job that became? The tech showed Zen how to attach the first blood vial to the IV tube, and she came back to switch out each vial.

More animals came and went over the next few hours. In between seeing each patient, the doc checked in on Weasely. When we had put all of Hoover's "donated" blood into Weasely's veins, it was just a matter of waiting to see how he responded. I carried Hoover back home. He had been curiously watching all of the action with great interest, seemingly having forgotten about his own ordeal.

In the cage at the clinic, Weasely seemed to be bouncing back slightly. He was less pale, he ate and drank a bit, and he even talked to us a little. He was always an extremely talkative cat — we swore he was sometimes trying to say human words. We would have whole conversations back and forth — one of the countless things about him that were so profoundly endearing.

We took him home in the evening, planning to bring him back first thing in the morning. *"Domani, controlliamo di nuovo,"* the vet said — Tomorrow we'll check again. We set him up with food and water and a nice pillow and blanket next to the *stufa*, so he could stay warm and comfortable overnight. The whole long night, Zen and I rotated between the couch and keeping watch over him on the freezing tile floor.

When we first started dating, many years earlier, Zen had two cats, Cleo and Meowie. I grew really close to them, and felt like I was their "dad," and I think they felt the same, but they were really Zen's cats from the outset. Shortly after we moved into our house together, Zen and I got Mr. Weasely from an animal rescue. A year later we got Coconut, another rescue, so that was four altogether. When Cleo and Meowie died a few years later (and a few years apart), it was extremely sad and painful for both of us. For all of us, I should say, as Weasely seemed to notice their absence as well. Years went by; we adopted Socksie, and later on Hoover, so we were back up to four. With each of the other three, Weasely had always acted like a father figure — showing them how to clean themselves, how to cover up a dump in the box, how to play and eat and snuggle.

At the time of our move, Weasely was our "elder statesman," as well as being our first "kid" together. He was also a living emblem of the sheer effort that we had put into keeping him healthy, despite seemingly constant medical challenges.

This is all to underscore the impact that this animal had on our lives, and how deeply we loved him. He was a huge personality, and a huge part of our lives together. So it was a fitful and fraught night, as Zen and I took turns trying to comfort our boy.

As the hours went by, we could see that Weasely was getting worse. His characteristic purr was absent, and his usually eager and happy face was haggard and stressed. A pitiful meow would come and go, when he'd slink under a bookshelf for a few minutes. He was clearly suffering, despite the day's efforts. Occasionally, Coconut and Hoover would nose up to him — they, too, recognized their big brother was distressed.

We made the decision sometime in the wee hours of the morning: We didn't want him to suffer anymore. We didn't want him to go through any more transfusions or operations or other procedures. We didn't want him to endure the stress or pain of a prolonged illness, as he had to do so many times in the past.

As soon as we thought it was a reasonable hour (it probably still wasn't), we sent a message to the vet tech. She wrote right away: *"Come sta Signor Weasely?"*

"Purtroppo male," we replied — Badly, unfortunately. We need the doctor to come and put him to rest.

We held him, petted him, talked to him. His soft body seemed limp, weak. We told him again and again what a good boy he was, and how everybody who ever met him loved him.

It was true.

Mid-morning, a knock at the door. The doc came in with his bag. We related the night's events. He checked Weasely over a bit. (He also took a moment to examine the other two boys briefly — they were both sniffing around his medical bag — and determined that they seemed in good shape.)

He agreed, in light of everything, that it was a good idea to end Weasely's suffering.

Zen held him as the doc administered the final dose of meds to put him down. As he slipped away, the doc checked him one more time, then made the pronouncement. Zen wept into his soft white fur and covered his face in kisses.

I walked the doc to the door and thanked him for his time and consideration. As he was walking out, he reached into his pocket and handed me a fresh pack of tissues.

Just then, Zen wailed, *"My boy!"*

Within 48 hours of us knowing that anything was wrong, our boy was gone.

The days that followed were a haze of grief and half-sleep, wine and coffee and tears. We rattled around our tiny apartment, not wanting to go out, not wanting to eat. Zeneba took the time to hide Weasely's medicines and toys and anything else reminiscent of him. I was usually the one who saw to his meds, and she didn't want me to be struck seeing this stuff repeatedly. Of course, Zen was inconsolably devastated herself — she alternated catatonic semi-sleep with fits of uncontrollable crying. It concerned me, the depth of her response to the grief.

In this week before Christmas, only two calls broke through our cloud.

One was from Floriana: She wanted to invite us to her mom and dad's place for lunch with the family on Christmas Day, before our concert at the retirement home. Celebrating was the last thing on our minds. We had probably planned to sit around feeling sorry for ourselves, then mope our way through our program at the Residenza. But this invitation to join an Italian family for their holiday lunch gathering was a huge honor, and not something that one turns down. Of course, we said, we'd be happy to come for lunch.

The other call was more problematic, and it jerked us out of our haze. It was our friend Sandy, who had been keeping our other cat since we left the US. We need to change our plan to bring her and Socksie to Italy, she told us. Various circumstances prevented her from leaving town any time in the near future.

That wasn't the biggest problem, though: "Socksie is really not acting well here," Sandy told us. "She's really aggressive and antagonistic to my other cats, no matter what I try." Though disappointing, this news surprised us not at all: We completely trusted Sandy's skill as a cat-manager, but we knew that Socksie could be hell on wheels. She was causing fights hourly, and Sandy just couldn't handle it for much longer. We'd have to find a new place for Socksie to go in the next few weeks, and Sandy would be unable to bring her to Italy at all.

Years of managing concerts in our chamber ensemble allowed us to develop a particular set of skills. Perhaps foremost of these was the ability to appear to remain cool while things went haywire around us. We engaged those abilities as we took this phone call: "Oh, that's fine, we understand, we know Socksie is such a pain, we're so sorry she's been so much trouble... No, no, don't worry, we really appreciate everything you've done for us so far, we'll get her off your hands as soon as we can... Okay, talk to you later, bye."

Click.

And with that, we immediately fell into a huge panic. In the wake of leaving Weasely, we didn't think that either of us had the emotional fortitude to take a solo trip to the States to retrieve Socksie. In any case, we didn't think we'd be allowed back into Italy on our temporary permit documents. Add to that our ongoing stress about finances — our house still hadn't sold — and this seemed an insurmountable problem. But we couldn't lose Socksie now, too. We had to get her out of there and over to us somehow. Zen retched a bit and tried to hold down vomit. When she gets incredibly stressed, she has a response of gagging.

After several hours of kicking ideas around, talking through possibilities and options, we decided to call another of our closest Nashville friends, Kristin.

"How would you like a free trip to visit us in Italy?" we asked her. "We'll buy the ticket, pay for your lodging, and pick up all your meals. Do you have a week to spare to bring us our girl?" Even as we presented the idea, we felt the strain of more money flowing out. We had already budgeted for this expense, and we'd set aside a large chunk of money to cover this cost of getting Socksie here. But given that our house sale was up in the air, we felt every drop of funds exiting our accounts. Nevertheless, we had to get our cat out of Sandy's place and over to us.

Kristin, for her part, was beyond excited. As she worked at a university, she had time off over the holiday break and into the second week of January. Within a couple more hours, we had arranged her flight for January 8 in the new year, a rental car, and her lodging. She and Sandy — two eminently professional and capable people — would coordinate handing off Socksie, and they'd also handle sorting out the relevant vet exams and necessary paperwork.

Despite the expense involved, this was a much-needed win, and our gratitude to our friends remains to this day. We'd get our Socksie delivered to us, as well as a visit from a dear friend — just not the one from the original plan.

Christmas Eve came, and we tried to rally ourselves a bit. Back in 2011, we had started a holiday tradition: Instead of giving each other material gifts, we collected little memories over the course of the year. Every so often, we'd write a little note on a piece of paper and fold it up and stick it in a jar. Each note would relate something that happened in our lives — a particularly interesting concert or meal or encounter, or even more mundane happenings in our home or in our town or in our travels. On Christmas Eve, we'd pour some wine, sit in front of the fire next to the tree, and read aloud to each other these notes. We saved them each year, planning to read them all together in one stretch, someday down the road when it was time.

Now we had the tree, though tiny. We had our notes, in a glass flower vase left here by the previous owner. We had the fire — well, a *stufa* pellet fire, anyway. Though neither of us felt at all festive, we thought we should proceed with our usual tradition of reading our notes.

It was a poignant activity. This year, in particular, had been such a whirlwind (obviously!), so there were a *lot* of stories. And we broke down in tears a few times as we went through the jar. Many of our little anecdotes were about our cats, and Weasely in particular: Some cute thing he did, or a bit about one of his vet visits, and how good he was to bounce back every time he got sick. It was more heartbreak all over again, but it was also a bit of a catharsis.

Around noon on Christmas Day, I packed up my guitar and we walked down the street, where Floriana picked us up to take us across town to the home of her parents, Maria and Giovanni. (It wasn't far, but we didn't yet know that neighborhood very well.) It felt strange, after a week of being alone with our sorrow, to hop into a minivan with Floriana and her partner and two desperately excited kids.

Maria and Giovanni's little apartment was packed — Floriana's parents, her partner and two kids, and her brother and his wife and their two children. Except for Floriana, no one spoke more than a couple of words of English, so we did our best with our Italian. It was chaos, but the most wonderful kind — the house was filled with excitement, joy, the energy of youth at the holidays. Delicious food, new presents, probably too much Fanta. Even in our still-raw grief, it was impossible not to be cheered in this environment.

When they asked me to get my guitar out, I obliged; but in the moment, I couldn't think of a single song to sing. No holiday carols, no funny ditties, not even a blues tune. My mind felt like an empty bucket. After sort of aimlessly picking for a few minutes, I put it away, and the moment was forgotten in the surrounding family hubbub. Zen eyed me worriedly. She could see I was struggling.

We had a lovely lunch — far too much food of course, but it was invigorating. We were abstaining (well, mostly) from drinking wine, as we had to perform later that evening, but at the end of the meal, Maria broke out a bottle of bright orange liquid. *"Mandarino,"* she said proudly, *"fatto da noi."* This was their own homemade *liquore*, from mandarin oranges grown in Maria's family home far to the south in Calabria. It was a common local product down there. Up here, it was liquid gold, tasting like summer in a glass.

As the afternoon turned toward evening, I saw Maria come over to Zen. We knew that Floriana had told her about our cat. She put a matronly hand on Zen's shoulder. *"Come va, Zeneba, come stai?"*

Zen was ready for such a question: *"Siamo triste a causa di nostro gatto,"* Zen explained, *"e anche ci manca nostra famiglia."* We were sad about our cat, and we miss our family on a holiday like this.

Maria pulled Zen over and hugged her. *"Oggi, io posso essere tua mama italiana."* I can be your Italian mom. Zen collapsed into Maria's hug and cried a little. (I might have cried a little too.)

Soon thereafter, we said our *Arrivederci* and our *Grazie mille* — we had to get going to prepare for the concert. As we headed out their door, Maria gave us a little bottle of *mandarino* to take home with us.

Now that we knew the way, we walked through town back to our house. It was getting dark when we got home. We grabbed our instruments (me switching my guitar for my cello) and a couple of music stands, and huffed and puffed as we hiked up the hill to the Residenza San Giorgio. It was a very steep walk, and bitterly cold. We were regretting turning down Floriana's earlier offer to drive us there.

The Residenza beckoned us from the top of the hill, with its cheery yellow lights and smoking chimneys. Formerly a fancy old hotel, now a retirement home, it was vividly dressed up for the holidays. The staff ushered us in and helped us set up to play in a big lounge room, where a log fire was burning in the hearth. Many of the residents were already gathered, and more showed up, curious, as we unpacked and tuned our instruments.

Over the years, the two of us had played countless duo concerts in any number of circumstances, sometimes under immense pressure. But neither of us could remember ever being this nervous. We had no idea, as we introduced ourselves in our best (but still a bit primitive) Italian, how these folks would respond to our music or to ourselves. At one point, in the midst of a really fun but difficult Baroque sonata, a woman's phone rang, and she answered it — loudly.

"Pronto?!? Non posso parlare, c'è un concerto!!!" I can't talk now, I'm in a concert. That was considerate of her, I thought. I smiled and looked over at Zen as we played. To my surprise, she was laughing! I had missed that smile.

A few minutes later, as I was introducing the next piece, another woman turned to the guy next to her and said (again, loudly), *"Non capisco niente lui diceva!"* I don't understand a thing he said! Zen and I both outright giggled at that. I guess my American accent was too strong. These moments really broke through our dark moods. It was nice to just smile and laugh at life after our past week. Notwithstanding the occasional interjections (there were only a couple of other phone calls), everyone generally seemed to appreciate the music, and their applause seemed genuine. And most of them appeared to understand our Italian, more or less.

Toward the end of our presentation, as we switched to a few familiar traditional Christmas tunes, we noticed that Floriana and her family had come to the concert — they were in the back of the room, smiling and singing along with the carols. Seeing them was another balm to our souls — reminiscent of our own family sometimes coming to our concerts in the States. And just like Maria had said to Zen, it felt like we sort of had our own family here in Italy.

These experiences encouraged us, but at this time of year, when the days are the shortest, it was easy to slip back into our sadness. And so we did — especially Zeneba. It occurred to me that, even though we were in this tiny one-room place, I felt like I saw her only briefly each day. It seemed like she was either crying uncontrollably — which was understandable enough, as I was feeling the same sorrow — or just lying in bed. I was worried for her general mental health.

Our friends Bo and Lee came to town a couple of days before the new year. They hadn't bought the house here that they were talking about earlier, but they had set up a five-year rental on a place up in the Rocca, and they'd be here for a month or so setting it up. It was nice to see them again — after all, they were the people who had pointed us to Soriano in the first place. They came by our house for a quick *aperitivo* early on New Year's Eve, and Lee had a little gift for us — she had lifted a photo of Mr. Weasely from our posts online, and they had enhanced and printed and framed it. That gesture prompted more tears, but it wasn't just more sorrow — it was a reminder that people still cared about us. They were on their way to a little New Year's event at a restaurant, and wanted to know if we wanted to come along. We begged off — not just for the money-saving aspect, but because we didn't think we'd be good company in public.

We both fell asleep well before midnight. Despite the visit from our friends, it was just another dark day to us. But we woke at midnight, the sound of fireworks cutting through our sleep. We tossed a couple of blankets around us and went out to the terrace. We had the best seat in the house for this show, the fireworks exploding into the sky over the castle. The terrace tiles stripped our body heat away through our bare feet; the steam from our breath lingered in the cold crisp air. I wrapped us up together in the blanket like a burrito, and I held her close, and we watched the bursts of lights across the valley. "Everything will be okay, *cara mia.*"

We had our appointment to go to the Questura on January 2 to sort out the next stage of our *Permesso di soggiorno*. Bo and Lee were kind enough to give us a ride into Viterbo. They dropped us off in front of the Questura and then went on their way to explore the town. Since we had been so out of sorts for the previous couple of weeks, we hadn't done our usual meticulous preparation for this appointment. But this particular meeting, it turned out, was easy, and our documents were fine — no misspellings, nothing missing. Even so, we imagined the prevailing mood on the day after a major holiday in an office like this would not exactly be jolly, so we approached the clerk behind the glass with our usual apologetic, grateful, cooperative earnestness. As it turned out, she was the one apologizing to us — she was sorry that the guy who needed to take our fingerprints hadn't arrived yet. We think she may have felt sorry for me also, as she noticed on our papers that it was my birthday. She suggested we go get a coffee and come back in an hour, and they'd sort us out.

There was a bar attached to the same building, so we took her advice. Though we had been assured that everything would be fine, we got a grappa along with the coffee — what Zen likes to call *"colazione di campioni"* — breakfast of champions. Suitably fortified, we returned to the office an hour later, and sure enough, they sorted us out quickly and easily. The main part of this stage of the process was recording our fingerprints — the guy smashed them one by one into a glass reader, as well as inking them up and getting imprints on paper. Then they gave us a few more documents, and sent us on our way. *Facile!* Easy. It was a nice day.

It got nicer still when we saw a message from our Realtor in Nashville. He was working with another buyer for our house, and an offer was forthcoming. We told him to keep up the great work — he knew our parameters, and moreover he knew that we trusted his judgment completely — but we were now cynically managing our expectations. Still, it was a glimmer of hope on that front.

A week later, Kristin arrived. We met her at the supermarket at the edge of town. She got out of her car, opened the passenger side, and... "Hi, Socksie!"

There she was, our little troublemaking kitten girl in her carrier. When she saw us through the screen of her carrier, she meowed indignantly. Kristin informed us that Socksie had been a perfect angel the entire flight, and seemed unbothered by the experience. The security people loved her, she didn't fuss the whole way, she never barfed or pissed herself. We had delayed her coming because we thought she would be the most agitated, but she handled all of it better than her brothers had.

We were also invigorated to see our friend, of course. Kristin was so excited to be visiting our little corner of the world. She knew our travel style very well — she had edited two of our small-town guidebooks — and she was looking forward to a nice week immersing herself in Italy, "Little Roads-style."

Kristin came with us to our place to introduce Socksie to her new home; then we helped get her settled into her apartment. It was the very same place on the *piazza* where we stayed on our first visit to Soriano — we had gotten it for an even better price than the first time!

It was a nice week. We took Kristin around the area to some

of our favorite spots, and explored others that were new to us. One was a 3,000-year-old pyramid deep in the woods, which had lain covered in vines and bushes, unknown for centuries until the 1990s. Then there were the stately Renaissance gardens and fountains of Villa Lante in Bagnaia, a little town just 20 minutes from Soriano.

While we were in Bagnaia, we noticed a giant conical stack of wood — some of the pieces as big as tree trunks — in the middle of the town square. At first we thought it might be a representation of a Christmas tree — we have seen tons of fun representations of Christmas trees in different towns over the past month. But we soon learned that this was a bonfire set up to celebrate the festival of Sant'Antonio Abate. We decided to return that evening for the ceremonies, as did hundreds of other people: A parade of trumpeters and drummers in medieval garb, followed by a solemn procession of priests. They carried a statue from one church to the other, a cardinal performed a blessing, and the bonfire was lit. It burned brightly — and *very* hotly — for hours, warming up the entire *piazza*. Members of the *vigili del fuoco* — the fire brigade— were everywhere, making sure nothing got out of control. Kiosks sold mulled wine; children ate special (and very large) cookies in the shape of a Pegasus; some guys managing a huge barbecue pit turned an entire roast pig for the crowd. It was a fantastic celebration — bright, warm, festive — hopeful for the new year.

On Kristin's last night in Italy, as we sat with *aperitivi* overlooking the valley, we got another message from our Realtor: It was done. The house was sold. We turned *aperitivo* hour into a celebratory dinner — this was a massive weight off of our shoulders, the last piece of the puzzle in sorting out our new lives. Now that we had finally reunited our "family" here, we were ready to get rolling with our businesses in earnest. We were already working with a good many travel clients — more than we had ever had when we lived in the US — and we had made a number of good contacts in the music and arts community in the region. We were confident that fruitful days were forthcoming in the New Year.

Early the next morning, Zen and I walked over to the *piazza* to meet Kristin for one last *espresso* before sending her off. "Let us know when you get checked in at the airport," Zen told her.

It was a foggy and chilly morning, and it rained as we walked, arm in arm, down the cobblestones back to our apartment. Despite the gray day, to us, it felt like a bright new beginning.

A couple of hours later, Kristin messaged us. "Dropped off the car, all fine. Checked in, checked bag, boarding pass in hand." We were relieved, especially with the foggy drive she must have had. We get preoccupied when friends or family are traveling to see us.

Then another ding from her: "Security was weird, took a while... Signs saying people traveling from certain cities had to stand in another line to do a special health check."

CHAPTER 9
Lockdown

*M*UCH TO OUR SURPRISE AND DELIGHT, Socksie's reunion with her brothers (two of the three, anyway) was not the hissing shitshow we had anticipated. She folded into the scene here as if it were no big deal — she just wanted to lie around with us as always. She resumed her favorite night-time routine — lying right in our faces while we're sleeping.

"If I'm lucky, it's her face whiskers and not her butt fur," Zen said.

"If *I'm* lucky, it's your face not mine," I replied. (I was indeed lucky in this regard. Socksie had always preferred to smother Zen, not me, and this had not changed.)

Cat butts notwithstanding, we went into February with optimism about the future. Now that things on the "home front" were sorted, we could really focus on our travel business, as well as reaching out to people in the cultural circles. We had a lot of irons in the fire. Projecting from our first two months of work, we had no doubt that we'd make our required income for the year to fulfill our work visa requirements.

A few weeks after Socksie got here, and with our house in Nashville sold, we felt free to get out on the road again, so we planned a trip up to Emilia-Romagna in February. We arranged for a couple to come and stay with the cats — a pair of traveling photographers from the Yukon who live out of their van for much of the year. The van was from the Yukon too — they had brought it across the Atlantic on a cargo ship, and now they drive all over Europe at leisure. As small as our apartment seems to us, it was an expansive palace to them, compared to sleeping in their vehicle.

With our cats in good hands, we headed north, to research restaurants and sightseeing spots and places to stay, and to celebrate a little, now that we felt things were on track. This trip expanded our offerings to travel clients, and also gave us the chance to revisit places listed in our guidebook to the region, to make sure they're still excellent. (Spoiler alert: They're still excellent.) It was our first research trip since we moved to Italy, and it felt strange — and wonderful — to visit these places that we had spent so many years exploring, which were now within a couple of hours' drive from our home. During the course of the trip, we uttered the phrase "I can't believe we live here" countless times.

While we were on the road, we had started to hear about a virus going around, in a couple of towns in the far north of Italy. Our understanding was that it was under control, with a couple of towns placed under localized quarantines. It seemed to be of little immediate concern to the people in the small, out-of-the-way places we were visiting in Emilia-Romagna.

We rented a car for that trip, and when we returned two weeks later, we concluded that we really needed to get a car of our own. We were starting to pick up gigs in various regions, and we wanted (and needed) to be able to travel for our business. Continuing to be without wheels, begging friends or neighbors for rides like a teenager, was untenable.

Over our years together in Nashville, we were always frugal when it came to car ownership. We'd never buy new, and never from a dealer. Zen had bought her aunt's Toyota Corolla for a dollar, and in hindsight that might have been priced a little high. Later we bought our Honda Element together, used from a neighbor, with cash. (Still later we sold Zen's Toyota for $250 to a junkyard — a huge profit!)

But now in Italy, we didn't think we could handle a person-to-person used-car transaction, between the language limitations and a lack of familiarity with the legality. After asking around a bit, we decided that we'd go to the car dealer in Soriano. They were well-regarded in town, a family business. Our adventure with the *stufa* had taught us of the value of doing things locally.

A vehicle on their site caught Zen's eye — a Fiat 500 (Cinquecento). These are among the smallest cars on the road. The classic Cinquecento models from the 1960s are those tiny clown-cars that appear in old movies set in Italy. The modern version looks like a clunkier VW Beetle. The one that Zen was looking at was a blue convertible, a couple of years old and with low mileage. This was absolutely not something that we'd ever have considered in the past — an impractical indulgence, a luxury feature on what was otherwise the cheapest car on the market. It seemed counterintuitive, as well as counter to our usual sensibilities.

But it was a cute little car.

First we'd need to find out if my cello could fit into it. If not, it was a nonstarter, and we'd be back to looking at the more sensible Panda models. So I carried my cello case to their lot to try it out, and to talk to the guy at the dealership about what we were looking for.

On my walk across town, my phone dinged repeatedly — messages from Zen, who built a compelling argument for the convertible:

Ding ... Maybe we don't always have to do the most practical thing

Ding ... a convertible would be so much fun

Ding ... Look at everything great that's happened by taking a chance

Ding ... We've done so many things very cheaply in this entire process

Ding ... Let's do something crazy!

Ding ... We budgeted a lot of $ for rentals over the year anyway, so subtract that from car cost

Ding ... Look at how cute it is

Ding ... Let's have a midlife crisis together

These were all good points, I had to admit.

At the dealer, I explained (with my American accent) who I was, what we were interested in, and why the hell I was carrying this cello case. *"È normale, no?"* Isn't it normal for people to size up a car by sticking an instrument case in it?

"Si, niente strano," the manager, Luca, shrugged with mock-casualness — nothing weird about that at all.

We walked out to the convertible, and he opened the trunk — just a tiny little hatch at the back. Again, it was extremely cute, but no cello would fit in there. I tried setting it upright in the front passenger seat, a method that works in many cars — but not in this one. Other customers on the lot stopped what they were doing to watch me wrestling with this cello case.

We put the back seats down and... *Voila!* I could see my cello would fit, along with Zen's violin, a couple of bottles of wine... and that would be about it. Good enough for us — where do we sign?

It turns out, buying a car was easier said than done. Though we were residents, the documents for our residency ID cards hadn't been processed yet — without which we were not legally allowed to buy a car.

But the everybody-knows-everybody system of a small town came to the rescue: The dealer made a couple of calls to the *Comune* to expedite our residency cards. What otherwise might have taken another month or three took just a few days.

Even so, the whole process took weeks, and during this period of waiting, we were growing increasingly agitated. After being restricted to doing everything on foot for over a month, and now that we had the other facets of our life sorted out, we were itching to be mobile again.

Adding to our agitation were increasing reports of coronavirus-related illnesses and deaths. It seemed to be spreading to other parts of Italy. News stories of overflowing and understaffed

ICUs trickled their way to our attention, but the information, though dire, was sparse and speculative, and the problems still seemed far away from our orbit.

MARCH 2020

In the first week of March, we finally got a message from Luca. The car was registered, tagged, cleaned and ready to pick up! We were so excited as he handed over the keys that we put the top down right away before driving it off the lot, even though it was technically still winter. It was the nicest car either of us had ever owned: It had windows that went up *and* down; a horn that worked; a chassis that didn't scrape whenever we turned left — unlike our previous vehicles. Not to mention the convertible top. It *was* fun.

We felt free, excited that we had achieved the Buy-a-Car accomplishment of our life in Italy. We got it just in time, too — that night we had a rehearsal in Umbria, about an hour away. We were invigorated as we played that evening. On one rehearsal break we proudly showed off our "new" car to the other musicians. It was nice to feel free and to be doing something so familiar again.

The next morning, Zen got a message from an acquaintance who lived in Rome. We had been planning to visit her down there in the near future.

"Too bad," the message read. "You should have come down while you could. :("

Wait, what...? Zen wrote back: "What is it? What's going on?"

"Coronavirus — it's now a pandemic. Full nationwide lockdown."

Well, shit. What does this even mean? We didn't know yet. We tried to get information from news sources, but it wasn't easy to find or to understand. The rules were nebulous at first;

the only thing that was clear was that we were restricted to our town, unless we had imperative reasons to go elsewhere. (We didn't.)

We did, however, need to go out for groceries. Our cupboards were pretty bare. In the States, we shopped less often and had a full pantry. Here, we shopped like many Italians do: a little here and there, this shop and that, nearly every day. We didn't even have a pantry, just a single cupboard for flour, salt, sugar, snacks, pasta. And that cupboard was mostly bare.

We walked into town for provisions, and we sensed immediately that the usual buzz in the *piazza* was different from normal. Police were out in unusual numbers, watching everybody. An older gentleman saw Zen and muttered something to her, gesturing to her face. He wanted her to put on a mask, and she didn't have one. Masks were recommended but not mandatory — yet. They were also not widely available.

A carabinieri officer approached two guys chatting in front of the butcher. *"Signori, c'è un'emergenza nazionale,"* he told them — Gentlemen, there's a national emergency.

One of the guys held up his shopping bag — *"Faccio la spesa..."* I'm doing the shopping.

The cop nodded. *"Si, hai fatto... ora, andate voi!"* Yes, you've done it — now go home.

The severity of this encounter cowed us. We had long been mindful to follow every millimeter of the laws here. Now those were changing quickly, and we were anxious to keep up, but it was difficult. Zen tried to cover her face with her scarf, in an attempt to "mask up." Aside from the authorities, it felt like the townspeople were watching each other as well — like an eerie paranoia drifting on the air.

Just then we got a ding on my phone: Our appointment to pick up our *permessi di soggiorno* had been postponed indefinitely, and there was a problem with Zen's file. What could that be? We tried to call but there was no answer. We sent an e-mail but we weren't optimistic that we'd get a response.

We did our own shopping quickly and headed back home. We gleaned that we were meant to keep our distance from everyone — including each other? We didn't know for sure, so Zen walked about 10 yards ahead of me the whole way, getting more and more stressed. When we got back to our apartment, I thought she was on the verge of a panic attack, jittery and breathing heavily. The uncertainty was excruciating.

The next day, we called our *avvocato*, who told us not to worry about our papers; we'd get it sorted out eventually. But whatever the document problem was, it would have to wait until we could be there in person — whenever that might be. We had read that personnel in the Questura offices were being reassigned to more critical duties during this time, so there was no telling when this kind of work would be handled.

The authorities urged people to stay in their homes unless absolutely necessary. *"Resta a casa!"* Stay home! It became a rallying cry. We learned through the town's Facebook pages that the Comune, in an effort to mitigate the pall of the restrictions, had declared a town-wide greeting: At 18:00 (6 pm), we were all encouraged to go out and cheer and chat with one another from our balconies or terraces.

At the appointed time, we went out on our terrace with a couple of drinks in hand and looked out at the countless windows and balconies of our neighbors. We chatted with Giuseppina and Pietro and several other nearby neighbors, and we waved to many others who were more distant. It was nice to think that people all around town were doing the same thing at the same moment

At one point people started exchanging shouts of encouragement to one another:

"Forza!" (Be strong!)

"Andrà tutto bene!" (Everything will be okay!)

"Resto a casa!" (I'm staying home!)

"Buonasera, Soriano!" we yelled back, wanting to participate. It was all heartwarming, even as it was frightening. We even heard a few people cracking jokes across the valley — we couldn't make them out, but we could hear people laughing in response.

Over the next two days, the rules were codified and tightened severely. We were now in a full lockdown.

Italy was the first country in Europe to implement a series of tightly regulated restrictions: No one in or out of their own town. No one could go out except for groceries (only once a week, only one person per household), pharmacy or medical needs. No lingering or gathering in the square or anywhere else. You could go out to walk your dog, but only within a limited radius from your house. Anyone exiting their home had to fill out an *Autodichiarazione* (self-declaration) form, stating who you were, where you lived, and why you were going out. Police were out in force checking the documents.

Bars closed. Restaurants closed. Hair salons, shopping malls, gyms, museums — *all* tourist sites — closed. You could go out for work, if your workplace wasn't shuttered. Theaters and concert halls — any of the places where we'd aim to do our work as musicians — closed.

At the supermarket, lines were monitored by a police officer, who allowed a limited number of people in at a time. Customers had to sanitize hands upon entry, then put on plastic gloves, and follow a prescribed path through the store. If you forgot something, too bad — keep moving through. The little food shops and the pharmacies stayed open, but only one customer was allowed inside at a time, and no extraneous chatting.

Carabinieri police patrolled the streets, making sure no one lingered in conversation more than necessary to complete a shopping transaction. And aside from the authorities, we continued to feel that the townspeople were watching each other as well. Or maybe that was only our own paranoia talking.

Masking was now mandatory. In the early days, improvised masks or bandanas were common, before proper masks were widely available. Zen crafted a couple from a pair of cloth napkins. *"Artigianale,"* Giuseppina said when she saw them — Artisan-made!

People were stressed, to put it mildly. Nobody likes to be told what to do and what not to do. But it was remarkable to behold the immediate sense of solidarity that the populace adopted here. We had all heard the horror stories of the deaths in the north, and no one wanted to risk that kind of wildfire spreading among their loved ones. Nobody liked wearing masks, either — who would? But virtually no one thought twice about wearing them. They were such an obvious and easy measure to reduce transmission. The images of refrigerated trucks arriving in northern Italian towns at night because the morgues were overflowing were also powerful motivators.

So everyone buckled down and followed the protocols, aside from the occasional dog owner who had discovered a new devotion to their pet's need for frequent exercise. One sunny day we coordinated a little long-distance game with our friend Floriana and her two boys. We can see their house in the valley from our terrace, so we used mirrors to flash sunlight and send "signals" to one other. It was a fun diversion for all of us — especially for her young children, whose childhoods would be forever shaped by this pandemic.

Despite occasional little glimmers of humanity, Soriano seemed like a ghost town. The usually bustling street across our valley was empty, except for the occasional Carabinieri car cruising, blue lights on. Every couple of hours, the local train from Rome cruised below our house and through the tunnel under the castle — almost completely empty. Occasionally, a car drove around blaring a tinny recorded message out of a speaker: Stay at home, wash your hands, wear your mask, don't gather, don't chat. It took on a dystopian feel: We could barely make out what the message was saying — it distorted as it bounced off the ancient stone walls and across the valley, reminding us of scenes from old war movies. It occurred to us that maybe the Italian community could take a crisis in stride so easily because of its long history of war-time. Perhaps it's ingrained in the national psyche. And the town's thrice-daily siren now took on a darker, more dire sound.

For our part, to say we were stressed is an understatement. All travel was halted at this point, as were all public performances or gatherings of any kind. This meant we could earn exactly zero euro. And though we were concerned about the money, we were much more concerned about not showing sufficient income to maintain our work status. On top of that, of course, we didn't want to get sick, and Zen worried that my asthma would make me more susceptible to a respiratory illness. And on top of *that*, the fact that our legal paperwork was up in the air indefinitely was maddening.

But with no way to resolve those problems for the time being, we turned our focus to something more positive. Seizing on the idea of the "town greeting" of the previous day, we decided to do a nightly concert on our terrace.

"We'll do one piece every night until the lockdown is over," Zen suggested.

"But we don't know how long this lockdown will be," I pointed out.

"Screw it, let's just do it," she pressed.

Her logic was compelling, airtight. "Screw it, indeed," I concurred.

We performed a different piece each day at 6pm, transmitting on Facebook live. After our second concert, our Comune got wind of our performances and asked us to adjust our time by 10 minutes: They wanted to broadcast us through the town's P.A. system in the square, but after they played the Italian national anthem.

So this became the routine: We'd start the day deciding on and practicing what we'd play. As evening rolled around, we'd set up chairs and music stands on our terrace, along with a lot of clothespins to secure our sheet music against the mountain wind. We rigged up Zen's smartphone on one of the stands, also with clothespins. This was a high-tech operation. At 6 pm, the cathedral bells rang out across our valley, then the Comune played *Il Canto degli Italiani* on the speakers in the *piazza*.

When the last notes of the anthem had dissipated into the air, we put on the most cheerful aspect we could muster, pressed "Play" and started our little concert.

"Buonasera Soriano!"

It became our concert title, our brand for this series. We'd introduce each piece in Italian and in English. Sometimes we'd forget to do the English part, but that was okay — we felt that this endeavor was really for the sake of our Italian neighbors, first and foremost.

We contacted the pianist Cristiana Pegoraro, an international performer who lived in a nearby town, to organize a collaboration. Each day following our own live performance, the Comune piped of one of Cristiana's solo piano recordings (of which she has many) into the *piazza*. We liked the idea that our neighbors could hear a "real" Italian making music, after our segment. For our part, it was nice to enjoy a cocktail on our balcony after we finished playing and to listen to Cristiana's piano tinkling across the valley.

Finding something different to play each evening was easy for us — at first, anyway. We had a wide range of duo repertoire to choose from, and we would sometimes throw one of my own songs into the mix — me on guitar and vocal, and Zen playing a "fiddle" chart that I hastily arranged.

The performance itself was sometimes more challenging. Playing what is essentially a single-take live broadcast always feels a bit dicey. Add to that some occasionally cold temperatures and an ever-present wind, and it became a nerve-wracking task. But each night, when we finished the final notes, we were gratified to see that some of our neighbors had come out to their own balconies to hear us, and they'd cheer and wave to us as we wrapped up the broadcast. When I did our shopping later in the week, the shopkeepers in the *piazza* would tell me that they'd heard us, and they appreciated what we were doing. And, of course, online feedback was instant and encouraging. That was enough to keep us going.

But some days, it was only barely enough. Even more than the technical aspects of these performances, the psychological challenge was often daunting. The streets outside were silent; the occasional train passing below was empty; the valley was eerily quiet, save for the sound of the sheep and the siren. Our own uncertainty over what lay ahead — for our own lives, and for the general future — cast a shroud over our moods. We'd take turns scraping each other up out of a daily depression as best as we could.

"Come on," I'd urge. "Sante's goats want to hear us play some more Johann Sebastian Baa-aaa-aaa-ach!" Zen would groan, rather than chuckle in response, lest she encourage more such punstery. But that sort of thing kept us going, in the face of both internal doubts and external discouragement. A couple of high-profile classical artists made public statements to the effect that musicians shouldn't be offering performances online for free during these lockdowns. Though we disagreed with that idea for a number of reasons, hearing these big names in our business suggest that we were cheapening the art with our little daily offerings was, as we say in classical parlance, a bummer. But actually, as the pandemic wore on, almost everyone in the classical world started using various online platforms to put their music out there — including some of those very same early critics.

Ultimately, our balcony concerts became a project that helped us get out of bed in the morning. The routine of it was something constant to focus on in these uncertain times, and we reinforced each other in the idea that we were doing something worthwhile, for ourselves and for our neighbors and other listeners. Zen and I had collaborated on so many artistic projects in the past, so we leaned into the challenge of this series of performances as something we knew we could accomplish — to varying degrees of success and quality each night, perhaps, but we did our best. The less-than-ideal conditions became part of the challenge. And sometimes it was even fun: For one night's show, I arranged (and we played and sang) Duke Ellington's "Don't Get Around Much Anymore," but we rewrote Bob Russell's lyrics:

> Don't know what day it is / Gotta go to the store
> Stocking up on our vino / Don't go outside much anymore

We heard from friends and family and neighbors who looked forward each day to our broadcast. In our own time zone, our show coincided conveniently with cocktail hour. We liked the idea that people were sitting down to listen to us with a Campari spritz in hand. And of course we'd do the same. Sometimes we prepped our own beverages ahead of time, so we'd be sipping them even as the delayed last few seconds of our performance drifted across to us from the PA in the *piazza*.

We sometimes set up a "virtual *aperitivo* hour" with a couple of friends. Lois (the violinist who we had worked with a couple of times before the lockdowns) and her husband Paul were avid fans of our *"Buonasera Soriano"* series, and they encouraged us greatly. These are two fascinating people: Lois is English, a tour guide fluent in Italian and expert in local history. Paul is Welsh, a scientist, craftsman, botanical photographer and author of 19 books on various scientific and artistic subjects. Now also Italian citizens, they've lived here for a couple of decades. They've restored an old farmhouse to create a beautiful rustic-English-manor sort of retreat in the Italian countryside. Though all four of us immensely dislike online video chat formats, our occasional WhatsApp cocktails were a huge balm to our souls. Like everyone during the pandemic, our sanity depended largely on various forms of virtual connections.

When we weren't preparing for each day's concert, we were doing our best to maintain our sanity, and also to find other earning opportunities where we could. I was commissioned to compose a piece for a recorder ensemble; Zen's vast array of contacts in the business yielded engagements with organizations to present online concerts. We did what we could.

Going grocery shopping became yet another project. The once-a-week, one-person-per-household rule was more like a recommendation than a hard regulation, but we wanted to present ourselves as model citizens as much as possible, so we took it to heart. I was more comfortable and accustomed to driving, so whenever we needed a larger load of groceries, it was me going in our car. Zen would make me a list according to the layout of the store aisles, so I wouldn't have to backtrack in the store, which wasn't allowed. When I returned from the store in the early days of the pandemic, I'd leave my coat in the car, and we'd wipe down all the groceries before I entered the house. (This was before there was a clear understanding of how the virus was transmitted.)

On my first grocery run during the lockdown, I came back with a large haul, including a lot of produce. This was not the way we wanted to learn about Italian fruits and vegetables. Before the lockdowns, we had been buying in the little local shops almost daily. We'd take the time to talk to the shopkeepers and other customers to learn about which fruits were best, which vegetables were seasonal and for how long, and how to select and prepare and cook everything the "right" way. Now, buying everything in larger quantities, we learned a lesson about Italian produce: It's bred and grown primarily for taste, and its shelf life is minimal. In the States, fruit and vegetables are grown primarily for durability and longevity. They don't taste like much of anything in comparison.

For years we had been used to stocking up a large amount of produce and counting on it for a week or more. Now we had to buy a large batch of produce, but we also needed to eat it all as soon as possible. A head of broccoli would turn yellow and bolt in three days. A head of lettuce would rot overnight. The first few weeks of lockdown, we learned a lot about how quickly fruit and vegetables rot here, which meant a lot of pasta with olive oil and chili peppers at the end of the week. Later in the pandemic, we got better at managing our shopping and cooking, but it was an adjustment.

Reading every day about the lack of response to (and worse, the outright denial of) the pandemic in our home country contributed to our stress. Knowing that deaths in the US would surely eclipse those in Italy made us fearful for our family and friends. A few of our colleagues reached out offering to help us, knowing we had been prohibited from working right after moving here. That was heartwarming, but also worrisome. We knew that US musicians, in particular, needed to prepare for their own work cessations. At one point, a former schoolmate reached out to Zen, saying that Newsweek wanted her perspective on our experience in this lockdown in Italy. Instead, Zen wrote an article about how we were much more concerned that the States should prepare itself for the same and worse, if leaders and citizens there didn't start taking it seriously. At the end of March 2020, Zen's piece appeared in *Newsweek*.

Around the same time, a reporter from *Il Messaggero* (one of Rome's big newspapers) contacted us, wanting to write an article about our concerts. Her English was about as good as our Italian, so we managed a dual-language conversation over the phone. That article appeared in April. We were glad that our neighbors could read, in Italian, how grateful we were to be in Italy, and in our town in particular, during this global crisis. We also hoped that the positive press might work in our favor with the Italian government, if we were unable to make any money and meet our requirements to stay here. We took turns staying up half the night chewing our fingernails to bloody stumps worrying about being deported.

APRIL 2020

"Buonasera Soriano!"

Day after day, our supply of new duo music dwindled. We had plenty of material, but much of it wasn't suited for the less-than-ideal circumstances of our concert series. Not too long or too short, not too esoteric or too quiet, not too many pages to keep from blowing off the music stand — the criteria were many and random.

"This sounds too much like a ringtone," Zen said upon trying out one piece. "Did Socksie write this duet?" she asked after we played through another. (Needless to say, those didn't make the cut.) We reached out to friends online, who provided us with ideas and sent sheet music. A few even composed or arranged pieces for us. On a few nights, one of us would play a solo piece, giving the other a night's respite.

In April another little project cropped up — not a paying gig, but a labor of love. We arranged and recorded a favorite song of Floriana's parents (who had invited us to Christmas dinner a few months earlier). At this point they were "celebrating" their 50th anniversary, stuck alone in Calabria, far to the south of Italy. Floriana and her kids crafted a video for them, using our audio as an introduction. It was the kind of project that kept us on our toes, and it lifted Maria and Giovanni's spirits, as well as their kids' and grandkids' — and our own.

The week before Easter, our Comune contacted us: Would we mind taking the weekend off, Thursday through Sunday, and resume on Monday? They were planning to broadcast Easter services over the weekend, some of which coincided with "our" time slot. At this point we had done 27 straight performances. Our commitment remained to continue our series every night until the lockdowns ended, but we gladly accepted this enforced break.

That Easter Sunday afternoon, we heard a knock at our door. *"Arrivo!"* I yelled as usual — I'm coming! We implemented our standard "Hoover-restraint-protocol Alpha" before I opened the door. It was a woman (masked, of course) with a gift basket in hand.

"Sono la cugina di Floriana," she said. This was Floriana's cousin, who runs an artisanal gelato shop in a neighboring town. She handed us the basket. *"Ecco un regalo da Floriana, per Pasqua."* An Easter gift from Floriana!

"Che sopresa, grazie mille!" we replied — What a surprise, thank you so much! It was a styrofoam container stuffed with three kinds of handmade gelato.

"Grazie a voi, per la musica," she responded — Thank you guys, for the music. It was gratifying to hear from another fan, especially one bearing gelato. Zen burst into tears at this expression of kindness. It buoyed us both to receive such a gesture from our friend in the valley. We were grateful, but it was just one in a multitude of gestures we witnessed in our community during this time. Leading up to Easter, a consortium of restaurants and individuals arranged to make seemingly unlimited Easter dinners, to be delivered to whoever needed them — people in quarantine, or elderly who couldn't manage to get out and shop. Though we were strangers to everyone here, we started to feel like a small part of this community.

We took the break from our concerts as an opportunity to plan out which pieces we'd play in advance. It helped to have a whole week or more of pieces lined up, so we'd know what and how much to practice each day. We resumed our concerts with a sense of preparedness akin to the kind of events that we used to organize in the States. It was reassuring.

And the reassurance was much needed, as the lockdown seemed to go on with no clear end in sight. The government made regular announcements, extending the restrictions a week or two at a time, based on the case numbers in various regions. It felt like it could continue indefinitely. Everyday life continued in Italy, but falling into a "new normal" that accounted for the many rules and restrictions. I dutifully filled out my *Autodichiarazione* form with each trip to the stores. I never lingered more than the moment it took to thank the folks manning the grocery deli counter or cash register for their heroism in coming to work every day so that we could eat.

One day in late April, I headed out to the supermarket with a big shopping list. On the drive to the store, the streets seemed even more deserted than usual — less standard pandemic and more zombie apocalypse. I pulled into a totally empty parking lot at the Co-op and saw a sign on the door: *"Chiuso il 25 aprile."* Closed for 25 April. I mentally face-palmed myself; I should have realized this.

Driving back home, I slowed down for a road crew re-drawing parking lines on the street above our house, and a pair of Carabinieri to manage traffic around them. They flagged me down with one of their dreaded red paddles.

"Dove vai?" a gruff, older officer asked — Where are you going?

I was going to do the shopping, I explained; now I'm going home.

"Dove abiti?" — Where do you live?

Just on this street, I said; 50 meters from here.

"Documenti, per favore." My heart rate spiked. While the guy took my documents — US license, car registration, and Italian ID card — to his vehicle, the other officer came up to me.

"Tutto chiuso oggi, 25 aprile — e un giorno festivo nazionale," she told me — Everything's closed today, it's a national holiday.

"Si, il Giorno della Liberazione," I replied, smiling in what I hoped was a self-deprecating way. I threw in an actual face-palm for clarity, and explained in my broken Italian that I knew that April 25 was a national holiday, but with the lockdown, every day seems the same and I didn't really know what the date was until I got to the store.

She smiled back. She, like everybody in these times, probably understood the idea of all the days running together. She turned toward her colleague, who was coming back to my car. She said something to him that I didn't catch, but then they both laughed as they gave my documents back to me. (I noted that they didn't ask for my *Autodichiarazione* form.)

"Buona giornata," she said, and her colleague waved me to move along. I quickly thanked them and slowly drove off, hoping I had successfully masked my shaky-handed panic.

I got back home empty-handed. Right away, Zen saw the still-shaken expression on my face. When I told her about the traffic stop, she just hugged me and patted my head. "You're okay, you're just such a hardened criminal, evading the authorities again," she teased. That calmed me down. Then she poured me a little glass of wine — that calmed me down more.

MAY 2020

"Buonasera Soriano..."

We continued our routine — checking the news every day for changes in rules or restrictions, preparing another piece to perform, occasionally running an errand. Every day did seem to run together into the next. But we were invigorated after our little Easter break, and the weather turned warm, which meant more people were out on their balconies regularly.

On the dirt track below our terrace, one of our neighbors in particular was a regular fixture of our life — an older *signore* who walked his little dog down there several times a day. He got used to our concerts as well, and one of his regular walks coincided with our 6pm performances. He'd linger down there every evening, waiting for the bells and then the national anthem. When it started playing, he'd stop walking, face the castle, and put his hand over his heart — it was an emotional moment for him and for us.

He'd hang around for our music as well, and his was one of the voices calling *"Bravi!"* when we finished each night. It was endearing. One night after we had finished, we chatted a bit across the three stories. I hoisted a glass of wine in his direction.

He grinned and pointed at my glass. *"Buon idea."* he said — Good idea. *"I medici dicono di pulire tutto con l'alcol."* The doctors said to clean everything with alcohol.

"Si," I responded, *"pulisco anche dentro il corpo."* I'm cleaning my insides too! I raised my glass anew, and we both chuckled at the idea. Then he excused himself so he could go home and pour his own "sterilization regimen."

Early one morning, Zen woke me up with her characteristic exclamation: "Holy shit!"

"What is it?" I sat bolt upright in response.

Apparently our *Buonasera Soriano* concerts had caught the eye of an American CBS correspondent who lived in Rome. He had sent Zen a message that he was producing a segment for *CBS Sunday Morning* all about people playing from their balconies throughout Italy. Did we want to be featured and interviewed? We were more than happy to participate, of course.

But this was easier said than done. The first question was, how would CBS get a camera crew here to shoot footage? The answer seemed to be: They wouldn't. Travel between towns was still prohibited, and the logistics of safety and permissions were, it turned out, insurmountable.

In the end, they decided they'd have to interview us online. But what about footage of us actually playing on the balcony?

No problem, they said — they could lift some clips from some of our concert videos, which were now archived online.

"But we need some other material, that we can use as sort of B-roll," they told us. "Can you guys shoot some video of daily life there? Practicing, kitchen stuff, laundry, whatever?"

I guess we could do that, we said, but we're not experienced with that sort of thing. We tried to manage their expectations. Zen shot some video of me making coffee and feeding our cats, who helpfully swarmed me one morning. I went down to the track below us to get a shot upwards toward our terrace. We asked a friend who lived in the valley opposite us to take a few seconds of video one evening while we were playing our concert.

The show aired on CBS in mid-May. It was inspiring to see other parts of the story, about people playing rock music above the Piazza Navona in Rome, or singing from their balconies in Milan.

Two days later, Italy announced a vast reopening and release from general lockdown conditions. I had arranged a version of *Il Canto degli Italiani* for this particular occasion, and we performed it for our last concert.

We had played 62 *Buonasera Soriano* shows in all, from March through May. This balcony concert series was an incredible gift to us — it had really kept us sane. But it was also a major challenge, and we were both exhausted. We decided to spend the first day post-lockdown, in self-imposed "quarantine." We wanted to get some good rest and be lazy, and we also wanted to see how the new rules — and enforcement — would look.

There were still a lot of regulations and restrictions, including those that governed public musical performances, so we were not out of the woods yet. But it felt like a hopeful time. The nation, and more specifically our little town, had rallied heartily to do everything possible to minimize damage during the lockdowns. We were really proud to have been a part of this community.

CHAPTER 10
Life After Lockdown

SUMMER 2020

*T*HOUGH THE HARD LOCKDOWN had been lifted, many restrictions were still in place, and so was the fear of infection. We had read so many stories about people who were being admitted to the ICU and placed on ventilators, and their families never saw them again alive. The government was beginning to distribute and administer vaccines, but we weren't eligible yet. They gave it first to the elderly and people with medical conditions that made them more vulnerable. It would be months before people our age or younger could get vaxxed. Despite the celebratory mood that came with the lifting of the lockdown, people still adhered strictly to the remaining regulations.

Restaurants reopened, but only for outdoor seating. Townships granted street space to restaurant owners so they could set up tables outside if they didn't have their own patio or garden space. Tables were spaced widely apart, and there were restrictions on the total number of people allowed, even outdoors. Italians were glad to get out, of course, but in May they still regarded the evening temperatures as a little on the chilly side. The result was a *piazza* strewn with tables at which three or four Italians sat, bundled up, as if they were part of an Arctic Circle expedition.

Bars were open, too, but also with strict rules: table service only, so no one could enter the bar except for staff. No gatherings of large groups, masked or otherwise, and espresso or other coffee could be served in take-out cups only, which was Just Not Right.

We ourselves weren't ready to visit restaurants or bars at first. "I'm not getting to where you're on a ventilator and I never see you again," Zen remarked. "I wouldn't even be able to curse at the doctors properly."

"There's no plate of pasta that's worth that risk," I agreed. Bathrooms were another factor. Normally, the use of a *bagno* would be simply the price of a quick caffè at a bar. Now that we wanted to avoid going inside anywhere, we stopped drinking liquids for an hour or so before running errands, to minimize the need for a bathroom.

Masking was still absolutely mandatory, even outdoors. At the entrance of every store and eatery was a hand-sanitizer station, the use of which was also obligatory. Police could (and did) issue fines for non-compliance with mask mandates, and citizens took it upon themselves to admonish one another to keep their noses covered and use the hand gel whenever entering a shop.

Each region was color-coded according to the prevalence of coronavirus cases. The travel restrictions and other rules varied according to color. We'd check the news daily to see which regions had changed to what color. A Red zone was essentially a full lockdown: restaurants, museums, and schools all closed, and no leaving town. An Orange zone allowed travel up to the borders of one's own region. A Yellow zone meant free travel within one's region, and also into any adjacent regions that were also yellow. It felt like a nightmarish Twister game in which the penalty for missing the color was a heavy fine and/or deportation.

Personally, we were still feeling a lot of anxiety about our future prospects in Italy. As the months progressed and rules shifted, we still had no travel clients. International borders remained closed, with only rare exceptions. Even when they did open, travelers from the US (the bulk of our clientele) wouldn't jump through the hoops it would take to get here, and they wouldn't like the Italian restrictions if they did. More importantly, though we were worried for our own futures, we didn't want to take the risk of encouraging potentially infected people to visit small towns (or any towns) across Italy.

It was also unclear when, and under what restrictions, we'd ever be able to resume performing. Gatherings at performance venues were still prohibited, even outdoors at first. So our earning potential was sub-optimal, to say the least. If we couldn't earn enough to live here, we feared we'd be forced to go back to the States. The idea was intolerable.

We decided that, regardless of the future of our work status, we should live our lives here to the fullest that we could manage, and hope for the best. If we weren't able to stay long-term, at least we would have enjoyed the short term as much as possible. So we started traveling again — little day trips, all within our region per the regulations. Fortunately, Lazio is a very large region, with countless interesting towns and sights within its borders. As the country progressed in reopening, we became more confident in the risk-prevention measures, so we felt safe to indulge in the occasional lunch in some out-of-the-way places. One day we enjoyed an outdoor meal (the only kind that was allowed) at a "km-zero" Slow Food restaurant in a tiny town perched up on a cliff. The town was famous for, among other things, a church with a reliquary containing the foreskin of Jesus himself — it's one of dozens of churches worldwide claiming to house this relic. Another day we traveled to a village whose walls are covered with colorful murals based on Alice in Wonderland, Pinocchio, Sleeping Beauty, the Little Prince, and a dozen other fairy tales. We even managed a quick overnight trip in a medieval castle right on the sea! All within an hour's drive or so from our house.

Some friends recommended that we visit a nearby *caseificio* — a cheese-maker's shop run by a family from Campania, the traditional home of the prized *mozzarella di bufala*. We found it on the map. The shop is in a service area on a highway leading directly into Umbria, which was off-limits at that point. So we plotted our route very carefully. We'd get off the highway at the service area to get our cheese, then take the very next exit, which had a pot-holed dirt track that looped around and under the highway, enabling us to head back home without breaking the regional border prohibition. It was a harrowing prospect, but we were assured that the mozzarella was worth the effort. (It was.)

In June, we got a message from the Questura in Viterbo: Our *permessi di soggiorno* were ready to be picked up. These were our permits to stay in Italy — and they bought us another year! Well, part of a year anyway — the 12-month clock had started ticking when we landed all those months ago — but we'd take what we could get. It was like a weight had been lifted from our psyches. Now it only remained to be seen if we could actually put together some work. Luckily, travel between some regions — including ours and the ones surrounding us — was now legal, augmenting our potential range.

Our collaboration during the lockdown with concert pianist Cristiana proved helpful now. She was restarting her long-standing Narnia Festival, in the neighboring town of Narni. This turned out to be among the very first festivals to reopen after the lockdowns, albeit with many limits and restrictions. Cristiana had exerted a Herculean effort in obtaining government permissions and assuring compliance with strict guidelines.

So she called us. She wanted us to participate in the festival. We were happy to play whatever she requested of us, of course. We proposed a concert of Italian baroque music — one of our favorite programs to present. She agreed to this, but she had another request.

"Yes, the baroque program sounds fine," Cristiana said, "but... could you also play a concert of American country and blues?" She had noted that our resumes indicated years of professional experience playing recording sessions and concerts with many big-name musicians of diverse genres, and it also mentioned my erstwhile identity as a guitarist-singer-songwriter. Cristiana assumed therefore that we could present a concert of

American pop music. "Italians would love to hear American blues," Cristiana explained, "but just keep it up-tempo."

Setting aside the oxymoron of "up-tempo blues" for the moment, we considered the offer. Other than the few of my tunes that we'd done during our *Buonasera Soriano* series, it had been years since I had played my guitar for more than a few minutes at a time. Nashville is home to hundreds of excellent guitarists of all styles, so my modest skills were almost never called upon. And Zen isn't trained in improvising in blues or country style, so I'd have to write charts for her for each tune, note for note, to emulate a fiddle-player sideman. For both of us, this would be far outside of our comfort zone.

So, naturally, we immediately agreed. "Sure, no problem," we replied. "Thanks, Cristiana!"

We hung up the phone. "How the hell are we going to farking put on a fracking farking country blues show?!?" Zen queried. *"Up-tempo blues?!?"* she added.

But these were challenging times, post-lockdown. We couldn't really say no to any sort of gig, farking or otherwise. We'd make it work, one way or the other.

And we did. Since we still didn't have travel clients, we had plenty of time to work up the show. I wrote a dozen charts for Zen to play, and we practiced for hours each day. In the summer heat, we kept the windows open all the time, which meant our neighbors could monitor our progress daily. Our neighbor Pietro recognized none of the tunes we played — he told us he didn't even know who Elvis was. The other neighbors occasionally offered a few compliments, and no complaints, so we counted that as a win. We alternated genres: 17th-century Italian music followed by American blues, rock, or country. (In Nashville, there are clear delineations between country rock, country blues, rockabilly, bluegrass, "newgrass," and dozens of other categories of music. We posited — correctly, as it turned out — that Italians wouldn't make those kinds of distinctions.)

Music festivals, and concerts in general, operate differently in Italy from the way they do in the US. In Narni, the "concert venues" are ancient churches, or Renaissance courtyards, or porticoes under a bell tower. A sacristy serves as a dressing room, and bathrooms are few and far between. And of course everyone is subject to the summer heat, mitigated only slightly by the cool, massive stones from which such medieval towns are built.

So it was that in July, we performed our Italian baroque program on a steamy summer Friday evening, in an 11th-century church lit entirely by candles. We had invited Floriana and Lois to join us for this performance, expanding our repertoire, and the sound of violins and voice spinning through the ancient space was magical. And performing live music again with valued colleagues, after being shut in for so many months, felt like a rebirth of our souls.

The next evening, we presented our American country-blues concert in Narni's *piazza* beneath the old clock tower. The tunes ranged from Elvis Presley and Stevie Ray Vaughan to Marvin Gaye and Etta James. As was traditional in Nashville, we attempted to get the audience to join in singing the last chorus of Kenny Rogers' "The Gambler," but to little effect. Though the crowd recognized the song, they were too polite (or too uncertain of the English words) to impose on our performance, even when we invited them to do so.

We also performed as part of the festival orchestra. It was our first time playing symphonic music since leaving behind our long careers as orchestra musicians. Because Cristiana's was the first festival in Italy to reopen, she had her pick of musicians from all over the country. Everyone was hungry to perform again, so it was an excellent and energetic ensemble. Doing this work that was so familiar, but in utterly different circumstances (not to mention a different language!) was strange but exhilarating.

The renewed prospect that we'd be working more meant that we'd need to be able to drive legally in Italy. We could drive here on our US licenses for a year; but after that, an Italian *patente* would be obligatory. First we'd need to pass the quiz (in Italian), which itself is notoriously difficult. From an array of 7,000 possible questions, the 30-minute quiz poses 40 of them at random. To pass, applicants can make no more than four errors out of the 40. And the questions are phrased in a way as to be deliberately misleading, tripping up even native speakers.

We were under time pressure to get our *patente*, too. Because of the lockdowns and subsequent regulations, the process of getting a license was much slower than normal. And to stay legal, we needed to get these things by the time our US documents expired. We were really starting to feel the stress of sorting this out, now that we were allowed to see to it.

A month earlier, we had started studying the 300-page bilingual driving manual, but we soon realized we'd need help. For one thing, the English part of the manual was exceedingly badly translated. In some places it stated exactly the opposite of the Italian text. For another thing, the logistical paperwork involved in signing up for and taking the test was complex, and we didn't want to risk screwing something up and delaying the process.

So in August we enrolled in the *scuola guida*, the local driving school run by Federico, a gruff but subtly funny guy in his thirties. It was a strange prospect for us to be going "back to school," and to be taught by someone younger than us. Funnier still: The class that we started attending several times a week was filled with kids ranging from 14 to 16 — the youngest ones, not yet old enough to shave, were striving to get their 50cc scooter licenses so they could tool around town on their *motorini*.

It was the two of us 50-somethings and a dozen adolescents who reeked of teen angst and Axe body spray, sitting in this classroom taught by a guy young enough to be my son. ("I guess that makes you the grandpa figure to these kids, then!" Zen pointed out helpfully.) We were glad that masks were mandatory, but even our FFP2 masks didn't quite filter out the smell of the kids' perfume and cologne.

Day after day we walked across town to sit in class. It was a tense environment, in part because of the shadow of the pandemic. Masks were still absolutely mandated at all times, and each of us was required to use hand sanitizer liberally upon entering the building. Federico covered a different category of questions each session, and gave us practice quizzes. We'd then review our errors in front of the class, and Federico would explain why our answer was wrong and how to watch out for that type of question in the future. We wondered whose anxiety was greater: Us two old foreigners with the weird accents, desperate to maintain our legal status after 30 years of driving, or the Soriano teens, desperate to get on their first-ever wheels and impress their schoolmates.

We started out pretty slow. It was common that we'd miss 10 out of 40 questions at one go, which would put us well into the "embarrassing failure" range. Although we were solid on vocabulary having to do with traveling, food, some history and politics, and, more recently, household stuff (gas supply, electricity consumption, estimates and invoices), we lacked some specific car and driving terms — brake, clutch, speed bumps, crosswalks, accidents, liability, criminal infractions, snow chains, reflective vest. We had a lot of catching up to do, but we did have the aforementioned decades of experience under our belts, which did sometimes work in our favor once we could sort out the gist of a given question. For instance, we knew that just because your car has an airbag doesn't mean you don't have to wear a seatbelt. We were, after all, alive when airbags and seat belt mandates were invented.

The class was a shy, almost disinterested bunch, but they seemed to perk up a bit when the two *americani* would interrupt with a follow-up question on a few points, based on our own years of driving in Italy. If we respect the speed limits, what do we do when the 10 or 15 drivers following behind us in traffic are getting angry because we're going so slow? If that sign means

"No Parking," why do we always see cars stopped there while their owners run into a bar for a *caffè*? When it comes to a safe following distance, what should we do when someone is so close to our rear bumper that we can't see their headlights? Federico's response to these questions was usually a shrug and a curt verbalization — *"B'oh!"* — roughly translating in this case to "Whaddaya gonna do?" But it was understood that, for everyone in this classroom, the rules were the rules — Period.

Enrollment in the class included a testing mobile app. Once we registered on that system, Federico could monitor every question on every practice test we took, which helped him know where to focus our study. Though we gradually improved our performance, we had bad days occasionally. One particularly depressing session — it seemed that every question had words in it that we didn't recognize, and so our error rate was terribly high — we stayed after class to talk to the teacher.

"Federico," Zen asked, *"siamo i peggiori studenti della classe?"* Are we the worst students in here?

He scoffed in response. Despite his mask, we could tell he was wryly smirking a bit. *"Guardate qua,"* he said — Look here — as he called up a complicated chart on his computer with a few taps on his keyboard. We saw our names on one of the columns — this was the practice test record for all of his current students.

"Ecco voi," he continued, highlighting our names on the list. *"Numeri uno e due della classe."* Here are you guys; one and two in the class. We were practically the teacher's pets!

In August, we organized more concerts, including two in our own town. In addition to the castle, Soriano has a palazzo with the most incredible Renaissance statuary and a mountain spring-fed fountain. This courtyard is an ideal setting for an evening concert — outdoors, plenty of room to space chairs, and an important and emblematic landmark of the town. Again we joined forces with our friends Floriana and Lois — at this point the four of us had established ourselves as a standing chamber group called *"Cari Musici,"* which means simply "Dear Musicians." Together, in collaboration with local museum officials, we presented an evening of music and poetry based on the moon. It was magical — Floriana's voice and that of the narrator wafting over the courtyard in the twilight, the sound of the water mixing with the flowing notes of the strings. Despite the masks and the limiting chair setup and the other antivirus protocols, this really felt like what we came to Italy to do: creating cultural events, and bringing communities together.

Floriana's mom and dad, Maria and Giovanni, attended the concert. Afterward, Maria came up to us and gave us each a big hug. (This was permissible, with masks.) They had finally returned to Soriano from their "exile" in Calabria, and it was the first time we had seen them in person since Christmas lunch. It seemed like ages ago.

We also returned to the Residenza San Giorgio retirement home, to play our country-blues show. Performing on their big terrace felt lovely to us, fresh and warm and breezy, but it was almost too chilly for the residents. We all soldiered through, though, and we all enjoyed a little celebratory *aperitivo* hour after we finished the show. The residents were more receptive to us this time — our language skills had improved since Christmas, and everyone was generally in a good mood, now that the darkness of the lockdown was lifted.

The owner of the Residenza gave us a gift as thanks — a huge crate of tomatoes from her garden. At this time of year, everyone had a tomato surplus, and we worked them into every menu at home. We made beef-stuffed tomatoes, rice-stuffed tomatoes, stewed tomatoes, tomato sandwiches, tomato caprese, tomato soup, tomato tart, tomato sauce, tomato salad, tomato pie, fried green tomatoes, tomato omelet. We got grape tomatoes, cherry tomatoes, plum tomatoes, beefsteak tomatoes, yellow tomatoes, purple tomatoes, blue tomatoes... Well, that's tomato season.

We had even tried to grow our own tomato plant in our window box, which yielded exactly one tomato all summer. Pietro walked by daily to chuckle at our pitiful attempt at gardening. And he responded, of course, by regularly giving us even *more* tomatoes.

Although we were now permitted to perform live concerts, we still had a few online engagements, as well. One was run by Naxos, the world's largest classical record label, which had released the Grammy-nominated first CD that we produced as directors of ALIAS Chamber Ensemble more than 10 years before. They put together a sort of "Where are they now?" online series. The answer to that question, at least for us, was unusual, to say the least.

AUTUMN 2020

Meanwhile, we were spending hours each day, week after week, reading and practicing for the *patente* quiz. To avoid feeling like we were back in lockdown, sometimes we'd drive up into the Faggeta for a walk, then sit on a picnic bench to study.

Zen is the first to admit that she's insanely competitive about almost anything, so anytime I outscored her on a practice test, she'd get alternatively mad or despondent. "I get that from my grandpa," she explained. "He would cheat me at Monopoly all the time when I was eight." But cheating was impossible on the app practice quizzes. It's hard to describe the matrimonial bliss of a married couple competitively studying for the same exam.

The competition was one thing; the pressure of the calendar was another. We knew that our international permits, based on our US licenses, would expire at the end of November. And the quiz was only the first step. Next would come actual driving lessons with Federico. Added to that was the news that the government was considering a limited lockdown period for the holidays, which could affect things like driving exam schedules.

But, *piano piano* — one thing at a time. We continued to attend our classes, along with many of the town's teens. "This is so weird," Zen observed. "These boys can't even grow beards yet, and meanwhile I'm sitting in this high-school desk with perimenopause."

I grinned. "Well, we can wave to those kids as we drive off after class, while they have to walk home." Age has that advantage, at least.

Finally in October, Federico decided we were ready. He gave us the paperwork we needed to take to the *Motorizzazione Civile* office in Viterbo — their DMV — where our quiz would be administered. Again, we were the oldest people there, even including the civil employees. A dozen computers were spread out in the testing room. We sat and took the exam along with 10 teenagers from all over the province of Viterbo.

When we were done, each applicant walked up, one by one alphabetically, to get the results. Zen was one of the first, and I could see that her heart was in her chest as the proctor reviewed her results on his computer.

"Allora," he said, writing a couple of notes on her paperwork. *"Promosso."* Zen sheepishly took her papers and exited the building — she didn't want to tell him she didn't know what that meant. I was the last one up, and got the same response from the proctor. I collected my papers and went outside, where Federico was talking to Zen. I handed him my papers. He glanced at them and said, *"Va bene, bravi."* Good job, you guys.

"Promosso," we know now, means "advanced" or "promoted." We had passed the quiz!

We each received our *foglia rosa*, the learner's permit, which is printed on pink paper. The teenagers who had come out of the same exam were grinning, too. Apparently everybody passed. But they regarded us with curiosity: These two old Americans are celebrating maybe a bit too emotionally. It was just a learner's permit, after all. *"Sono più orgoglioso di questo che della mia laurea!"*

Zen exclaimed to Federico — I'm more proud of this than of my college degree! His eyes smiled over his mask — he probably knew that while the rest of his students would celebrate over a Fanta at McDonalds, we would head to Luigina's, where we'd review each other's errors over a couple of *negroni*.

In the meantime, we had organized several more fall concerts with our chamber group, including one in a nearby town at a stunning Renaissance *palazzo* once frequented by Galileo. Some of the rooms were outfitted with displays of his papers and globes and scientific experiments. It felt like Galileo might walk in at any moment, as if he had just stepped out for an espresso. These kinds of experiences made us stop and marvel at how lucky we were to live in a place so rich in history and beauty. Doubly so when we had the privilege to perform Italian baroque music in these ancient spaces. The toughest part of gigs like these was keeping ourselves from rifling through all the closets and drawers in the "green room" spaces we were provided, which were rooms in these *palazzi* that are usually closed off to the public.

Halloween arrived. Italians recognize that this is a big day in the US, and they seem to have gradually tried to incorporate a few of the elements of the festivities. Kids dress up in costumes, sometimes in connection with public events in town squares, but by and large, the door-to-door trick-or-treat idea seems to be regarded as perhaps a bit *too* foreign. In any case, no large gatherings or celebrations were allowed this year — part of the ever-shifting pandemic restrictions.

Nevertheless, we decided to dress up in costume ourselves and drive over to Floriana's house to take bags of candy to her two young boys, who, like the rest of the local youth, were precluded from getting together with friends. We went to great lengths to find several bags of purple and green balloons. We blew them up and fastened them to our sweaters so we'd appear to be, we hoped, a big bunch of grapes and olives, respectively.

They were not the best costumes. In fact, we looked downright ridiculous.

"You look like the Fruit-of-the-Loom guy!" Zen quipped. "They're going to think we're marketing underwear."

"I think we're safe," I replied. "I don't think they have that brand here."

Driving with balloons bursting out of the convertible top of our tiny *Cinquecento* surely violated several of the motorist rules we had just been quizzed on. But we managed the five-minute drive to Floriana's house, where the kids were already waiting in the yard in their own costumes.

"Trick or treat," they called out in English, trying to sound scary. (They didn't.) They were oblivious to the fact that this whole operation was backwards from the standard Halloween activity. *We* weren't supposed to dress up and come to the door. *They* weren't supposed to say "trick or treat" when *we* showed up. *We* weren't supposed to take candy to *them*. But they didn't care — it was all great fun to them, especially after some nine months of great uncertainty.

They were puzzled at first at our costumes, until we explained: *"Siamo uve e olive!"* We're grapes and olives! They burst out laughing, their high-pitched child-laughs echoing through the olive grove that surrounds their home. They seemed to appreciate our effort to recognize these two iconic elements of Italian food culture, no matter how goofy we looked doing it.

Now that we were the proud holders of the *foglia rosa,* our next hurdle was driving lessons with Federico. Each of us had to do 12 half-hour sessions with Federico before we could drive for the examiner. For two "old" people, this should have been no big deal. But Zen hadn't driven much at all, other than her scooter in Nashville, for close to 10 years, so to say she was out of practice would be an understatement. Between Federico's gruff edges and her lack of confidence with the language, she frequently got nervous and therefore hesitant, which is definitely a drawback when driving in Italy. Moreover, the most frequent words used in these sessions —*freccia, frizione, freni* (turn signal, clutch, brake) — all sounded a little too similar to one another in the heat of the moment.

"These are not the F-words I'm good at," Zen said.

For my part, though I was comfortable enough driving, I faced challenges of my own. When another driver stopped in the middle of the street, or someone at a stop sign failed to demonstrate the "stopping" part, I'd hold up my hands in a "WTF" gesture.

"No, no, Matt," Federico admonished on my first couple of sessions. *"Non gesti con le mani."* Don't gesture with your hands!

Zen thought this was hilarious. "I can't believe," she snarked on our drive home that day, "that the WASPiest, most rule-following-est Boy Scout of all time got busted for gesturing with his hands... in ITALY!"

Zen dreaded the prospect of failing the driving test. We had dumped a ton of money and time into this endeavor, and so much depended on succeeding. Driving away after one particularly bad session (in which Federico questioned why she was driving with such a lack of confidence that day), Zen asked me to pull over. I did, and she got out and barfed in the bushes by the road.

But, as always, she soldiered on through the challenge. In December, we drove for our test with the examiner, along with a half-dozen of Federico's other students. Everyone was masked — the examiner in the back seat, Federico sitting shotgun, and each of us driving in turn. This part ultimately proved much easier to manage than the quiz had been. I did my best to drive like a *pensionato* (a retiree), never going faster than a second-gear speed throughout town. Though it might have taken a bit longer than the examiner preferred, he passed me and handed over my shiny new *patente*.

Zeneba was next. I got out of the car and she got in, and I

paced around outside the school when she drove off. I was more anxious for her than I was behind the wheel myself. Ten minutes passed, then 15. A few of the other students were waiting for their turns, and I wondered if they felt as I did, like an expectant father pacing in a hospital waiting room. (Considering that they were all 16 years old, I doubted it.)

Finally the *scuola* car pulled up, and through the windshield I could see her body language and Federico's. She got out of the car and held up the pink license — *"Promosso!"* she exclaimed with a grin. (She was still masked, but I can recognize her smile based on any part of her face at all.)

"Everything was fine, except I parked like an asshole," she said as I gave her a big congratulatory hug. Then she whispered in my ear: "Let's run away, before they change their minds!"

We received our *patente di guida* just over a year after we moved to Italy, and just a couple of weeks before another lockdown that would have prevented us from continuing our schooling. Despite the challenges of the previous 12 months — quitting our jobs and downsizing our life, moving to another continent, coping with the global pandemic and the resulting paucity of employment, handling a hundred little challenges and a few huge ones — we had done everything that we had set out to do. Getting these licenses felt like the last milestone in the process. We were now really free to live our lives in Italy.

Epilogue

"*C*OME, CHILDREN!" Floriana called in her singsong English; then in Italian: *"È l'ora di trovare le uova Pasquale!"* Time to find your Easter eggs!

The sun shone down on the olive grove that surrounds her home. Little wildflowers filled the air with a sweet scent of spring. The four youngsters — Floriana's two kids and their cousins, her brother's children — came running through the olive trees and swarmed around Floriana. Her dogs, Musetta and Stella, ran up to join the gaggle, tails wagging wildly.

When she had the kids' attention, Floriana read to them a series of rhymes that she had crafted herself — clues to the hiding places of the eggs placed around the grove. As the cousins scattered to begin the hunt, dogs on their heels, Floriana's brother appeared and produced a treat for the adults as well — a fresh bottle of prosecco, to enjoy with the end of the Easter lunch. The previous trays of food — an unreasonable quantity of cannelloni, grilled vegetables, and pork chops — had been cleared from the garden table, making room for a wide array of cookies and cakes. The star was the *colomba,* a traditional candy-covered bird-shaped cake, the Easter counterpart of the Christmas *panettone.*

While the kids gleefully careened from one hiding place to the next, we sat with Floriana, her brother and his wife, and their parents Maria and Giovanni. Over the past couple of years, Maria had made good on her promise to be our "Italian mom." She came to all of our local concerts, clapping especially loudly even when Floriana wasn't singing with us. She made lots of edible (and drinkable) treats for us — cookies, hot dishes, *mandarino liquore*. She even invited us to her family's homestead far to the south, deep in the countryside of Calabria.

And now, here we were, joining them all for Easter lunch. It was two and a half years since we had gathered with this same gang at Maria and Giovanni's house on our very first Christmas in Italy. It felt like a lifetime ago.

The family was exceedingly kind about our still-halting Italian. *"Piano piano,"* Floriana's brother declared. *"Siete molto migliorati da quel Natale!"* You've improved a lot since that Christmas!

They all reassured us that our near-constant errors and mala-propisms were merely *carino* — "cute" — rather than *stupido*. (This was a common and very charitable response to our efforts to speak Italian.)

In any case, our conversations were lively and varied, com-peting with the outbursts of the cousins' voices from the grove and the occasional dog bark weighing in. We told them about the concerts we had been doing since the lockdowns and restric-tions had lifted — performing in Chianti vineyards and castle courtyards. We heard stories about how the kids were doing in school now that they were back to in-person education. We related anecdotes of our travels of the past year, from our excur-sion to the Dolomites far to the north, to our adventure in the fruit-laden enclave of their own family in Calabria.

The two of us sat back as the family engaged in a heated debate about which was the best bakery on the Tyrrhenian coast. We had an extended discussion wherein we attempted to describe a Chicago-style deep-dish pizza. (They made us repeat ourselves several times; they couldn't believe that what we were talking about could possibly be a real thing.) We told them that, now that international travel had opened up again, we had resumed making itineraries for clients. Life was approaching a "new normal," and bit by bit our opportunities had been improv-ing.

"Piano piano," Giovanni sagely observed.

Later in the afternoon, after we had all eaten as much as we possibly could, the kids and the parents — and Zen and I — gathered in the yard to play a game, new to us, that involved tossing and knocking over a series of wooden blocks. Zen and I struggled to keep up with the rules, so we frequently stepped aside for a little extra sip of something.

I noticed that Maria and Giovanni were sitting back on a bench, proudly watching their family as they leaned against one another, arms entwined. I put an arm around Zen in the same way and nodded in their direction. She looked at them, and we both grinned, overwhelmed by the kindness that this family — this town, this country — had shown to us these past couple of years.

Zen held up her glass, and I clinked it with mine.

"I can't believe we live here," she said.

ACKNOWLEDGEMENTS

So many people have helped us, logistically or emotionally, to realize this seemingly impossible dream. Many of those people are mentioned in this book. Two in particular did not appear, but we owe them a great debt: Lea and Justin.

We would also like to thank our family, who supported us in this endeavor even though it meant being separated by an ocean.

Finally, we want to thank our neighbors of Soriano nel Cimino (again, many of whom are mentioned in the book), for welcoming us so warmly into their community. *Grazie mille, carissimi vicini!*

Little Roads Europe Travel Guides

In addition to their decades-long career as Grammy-nominated performers, record producers, and concert organizers — which continues in Italy to this day! — Zeneba and Matt are also the authors of four award-winning guidebooks. These travel guides explore the small towns, back roads, traditional foods, and expansive history of Ireland as well as Tuscany, Emilia-Romagna, and Italy's Alpine Lakes.

Visit LittleRoadsEurope.com

CPSIA information can be obtained
at www.ICGtesting.com
Printed in the USA
BVHW082115030423
661653BV00001B/64

9 781088 021255